My Beautiful Sisters

My Beautiful Sisters

A Story of Courage, Hope and the Afghan Women's Football Team

KHALIDA POPAL

JOHN MURRAY

First published in Great Britain in 2024 by John Murray (Publishers)

1

A CIP catalogue record for this title is available from the British Library

Hardback ISBN 9781399805728
Trade Paperback ISBN 9781399805735
ebook ISBN 9781399805759

Typeset in Monotype Bembo by Manipal Technologies Limited

Printed and bound in Great Britain by Clays Ltd, Elcograf S.p.A.

John Murray policy is to use papers that are natural, renewable and recyclable products and made from wood grown in sustainable forests. The logging and manufacturing processes are expected to conform to the environmental regulations of the country of origin.

Carmelite House
50 Victoria Embankment
London EC4Y 0DZ

www.johnmurraypress.co.uk

John Murray Press, part of Hodder & Stoughton Limited
An Hachette UK company

To the fighters, survivors and advocates for women's rights as human rights, may we continue to empower and uplift each other.

Some people believe football is a matter of life and death. I am very disappointed with that attitude. I can assure you it is much, much more important than that.

Bill Shankly

Women's sport is neither appropriate nor necessary.

Ahmadullah Wasiq, Deputy Head,
the Taliban Cultural Commission

Author's Note

To protect the privacy of those in Taliban-controlled Afghanistan, I have changed the names and identifying characteristics of some individuals. Despite these changes, this book is an entirely authentic representation of my experiences.

This book contains descriptions of sexually abusive behaviour and suicidal ideation.

Prologue

Melbourne, August 2023

The same images are always there, waiting for the moment when I close my eyes. A knife slicing into a ball. Men laughing, their faces hateful. A helicopter's blades spinning, dragging smoke behind them. Blood dripping slowly into the dust. The silhouette of a girl twisting in flames.

'Khalida?'

I open my eyes.

I nod to the woman who is organising the event and take a breath.

It is the day before the Women's World Cup Final in Sydney, and I am standing to the edge of the small indoor pitch at the back of the Ultra Football store in Melbourne. In front of me are members of what used to be the Afghanistan women's national team. It would not be an exaggeration to say that it's a miracle any of us are here to tell our story.

Tomorrow, the world will be watching as the best women's national football team in the world is crowned. But not every team was able to compete. The Afghanistan women's team remains unrecognised by FIFA, football's global governing body. The irony that the World Cup is in Australia this year, where the majority of the Afghanistan women's team fled to as refugees when the Taliban returned to power in August 2021, immediately banning all women's sport, is not lost on anyone.

Nor is the fact that the men's team is recognised and continues to compete.

I have been flown here from Denmark, where I have been living in exile from Afghanistan for more than ten years, by Malala Yousafzai, the Nobel Peace Prize-winning education activist. I did not need to explain to her what it is like to live as a woman under a repressive regime. What happens when the men to whom you have become an annoyance decide to swat you like a fly. So here I am, to be reunited with my sisters and introduce her to them. To help tell the story of the team to anyone who will listen. But where does the story begin?

Almost exactly two years ago, I had watched as the reports came in that Kabul had fallen back into the hands of the Taliban. Then the calls started. Not just calls: voicemails, emails and messages through every channel online. Even though I had been away from Afghanistan for more than eight years, as it was not safe for me to be in the country, I was still one of the most high-profile figures there in women's football, so as the storm broke, I was a lightning rod. I surpassed WhatsApp's capacity for incoming content three times in one day. Not only friends, family, former teammates and players I had worked with were sending me messages, but also players who I didn't know, teenagers and girls in their early twenties who had begun playing long after I had left Afghanistan, who had never experienced life under the Taliban.

I received a call in the middle of the night. When I answered the phone, I heard a quiet, hoarse voice. It was a woman. She whispered in Dari, 'Is that Khalida?'

'Yes.' My throat was dry, my eyes burnt as I tried to wake, unsure if I was still dreaming.

'I have my brother's gun. I'm sitting in front of my window, watching outside. I haven't slept. When they knock on my door, I will shoot myself in the head. It is better to kill myself than be caught by them.'

I knew then that this was not a dream.

'Where are you?' I asked. Taking down her details, I added her name to my list and told her I would call when I knew more. My desk was full of half-empty cups of coffee. I couldn't remember the last time I ate.

Like many of us who had escaped, I naively thought that my country would never be abandoned by Western forces. We believed that the damage to their reputations if they surrendered to the Taliban and withdrew their troops would be enough to prevent them leaving. We believed we were safe. We were wrong.

We watched, first in disbelief and then in horror, when the US government, led by Donald Trump, signed a deal with the Taliban in February 2020. The US and Nato allies agreed to pull all troops out of Afghanistan within fourteen months of the Agreement for Bringing Peace being reached. On 12 September 2020, a group of twenty-one members of the Afghanistan government gathered in Doha, Qatar, to meet with twenty-one representatives of the Taliban for 'peace talks', to discuss the future of the country after the withdrawal of US troops. There were only four women in the room. The Taliban did not greet them or make eye contact.

Over the coming weeks and months we heard that the Taliban were winning. The Afghanistan government, which had been installed by the US, were cut out of the peace talks altogether and the US government was negotiating directly with the Taliban. Schools were closed. International allies were starting to give up and Western powers were leaving the country.

My organisation, Girl Power, runs grassroots football programmes in a number of different cities and provinces across Afghanistan. The coaches and players were telling me that it was becoming increasingly unsafe to be there. As the Taliban advanced, I advised them to bury their football shirts, their trophies and any photos of themselves playing football, erase their histories and get to Kabul. The fighting had escalated and was almost continuous as the Taliban moved from rural areas into the cities. In April 2020, we had had to cancel a football event for girls in Jowzjan province, a rural area in the north of the country, because war had reached the region. The government had lost power. Mothers of the players I spoke to were terrified of sending their daughters to school, fearing they might not come home. The temporary president of the Afghanistan Football Federation warned the women's team to stay away from the federation's offices and facilities, to stay away from the pitches, because it would create too many problems between the federation and the Taliban, and he didn't want anyone at the federation to be killed because of them.

We waited in hope for the government to fight back. Then we heard that they were surrendering, ordering military leaders to tell soldiers to give up their guns, actively preventing them from fighting back. There were videos of soldiers in tears, begging to stay armed and do something. I had relatives and friends in the military who had their guns taken away. They were forced to stop fighting, and because of that they lost their lives. They were betrayed by their own leaders and their supposed allies.

And then, in August 2021, Kabul fell.

Drivers, translators, cooks, teachers – anyone who had connections to international nations with troops in Afghanistan – were now in immediate danger. I found myself explaining what life under the Taliban was like to people who were not familiar with it: that all forms of entertainment were forbidden and why new members of the Taliban, neighbours and men locally that were either supportive of the ideology of the Taliban or who joined out of fear, were going door to door asking for the names of women football players.

They smashed ancient statues, musical instruments and televisions, burnt movie reels and music tapes on huge pyres. They did not ban football completely. Men were able to go to the stadiums and watch a match, but the sport was now prohibited for women. Anyone who had been caught stealing would have their hands slashed at the football stadium in a public display of punishment. Those sentenced to be executed were hung from the goalposts, left swaying above the grass.

The Taliban rule with the belief that women should not be educated, not be permitted to work or play any sports. Those of us who had played football in Afghanistan after the Taliban had been driven out in 2001 were automatically targets of persecution by them. Many of the players had been vocal in the press, using the small platform football had given them to speak up on women's rights. They had been visible in their communities as actively flouting everything the Taliban believed, and they were now in imminent danger.

They had to go into hiding. The Football Federation did not respond in any way to safeguard the players, and few people could be trusted to help, because any chance to ingratiate themselves with the Taliban could lift the pressure and eyes off their own families. We had to get the women out, and I felt a particular responsibility to save them because I felt like their exposure was my fault. I had set things in motion when I started the Afghanistan women's national football team, all those years before.

Back then we were told that Western powers had swept the Taliban out of power in the name of human rights. For women's rights. To protect and stand with the women of Afghanistan, in the face of a regime that crushed them. And so, we had thrown ourselves fully into the fight for an equal society, and the vehicle for our fight was football. Despite facing backlash many times, we persisted. We did not hide our faces. We did not stop photos being taken of us or our stories being told, because we felt the hand of the world on our shoulders. We became symbols of courage and endurance to other women. We were a team.

We spoke our minds. We advocated human rights and contradicted the core beliefs of the Taliban over and over and over again.

Now they were back in power and we were a threat, targets to be silenced once and for all. The familiar face of oppression loomed over us, over all of the women and girls of Afghanistan, and what we had to lose was our freedom, our voices, our lives.

'Khalida?' the event organiser says, snapping me back into the present.

I take a deep breath and open the door. Time to tell our story.

I

Kabul, 1996

There is the ball and there is you. There are your feet, kicking the ball. There is the ball and there is the breath moving in your lungs. Your legs moving you over the ground. As soon as you kick the ball it is like magic. You are smiling. You are in control. You can ignore the eyes watching you, the voices calling out. It is just you and the ball. Open your eyes.

'Khalida! Khalida!'

One of the neighbourhood boys was waving his arms, calling for me to kick the ball to him, but I kept running. He stopped, frowning. I kept running, my breath loud in my ears. I made to pass one way, then cut back. If you had asked me why, I wouldn't have been able to tell you – it just felt right. Running and running, until I finally lost the ball and stood panting, smiling.

'Khalida!' My brother Shapoor's voice was deep and serious. Even though he was only eight years old, a year younger than me, he acted like he was older. 'We have to go home.'

I pulled a face. 'Just a little longer?'

He shook his head firmly. 'I promised Mum and Dad I'd get you back on time. Tonight is the wedding. You have to go with the women. They are going to make you *beautiful*.'

I stuck my tongue out and hit him on the shoulder and we began the short walk back to our house.

It was a beautiful late autumn afternoon in Kabul and I was happy to be outside. Only a couple of years before, we had been forced to live in our basement for months, sheltering as different groups battled for control of Kabul. We had huddled in a corner of the room, padded with cushions, blankets and mattresses, listening to the explosions outside like distant thunder. To distract us my father would read out the most interesting facts from whatever history book he was reading. I would lie with my head on his chest, listening to the sound of his heartbeat as I drifted into sleep. The fighting eventually receded, but there were still piles of rubble left around the city. Our neighbourhood, Khair Khana in Kabul, had been spared the worst of the damage. I hadn't really understood what was happening at the time; all I had known was that I was furious I couldn't go to school. I still flinched if someone let off a firework, or an engine backfired in the street outside.

Shapoor and I stood to the side of the road to let a woman in a burqa pass by. She stopped, looked at me and gestured vigorously towards her head. I realised that I had taken off my scarf earlier to play football and forgotten to put it back on. I hated wearing one, especially when it was hot, but I pulled it out of my bag and tied it around my head.

There had been more and more of these strange dark shapes moving around the streets over the last few months. We knew that out in the countryside, a group known as the Taliban was growing more powerful. Adults would crowd around the television, shaking their heads as distant cities were taken over. But in Kabul, the change was measured in the presence of those dark shapes, in the shaking of heads or tutting, or comments muttered under a person's breath.

My family were not religious; the focus was more on education in my household. My grandfather was a university professor who had spent a lot of time travelling around the world. My grandmother was one of the first women to graduate from school in Kabul. My dad came from a very westernised, liberal-minded military family that valued education above all. When I heard the adhan, the call to prayer, echoing through the streets of Kabul from the top of every mosque in the vicinity, I would watch, bemused, as men, women and children trudged to pray while I continued to play. We never answered that call. My parents didn't use the term 'atheist', but, essentially, that's what they were. They didn't go to mosque, they didn't pray, they didn't practise any religion. Instead, my grandparents and, in turn, my parents talked about the importance of family, good values, respect, transparency, honesty and being there for each other. We were taught to stand up for what we believed in, to speak up and take action if we saw something that was wrong.

Like all the men in his family, my father was tall and broad-shouldered, loud and charming. He would stand preening in front of the mirror at his appearance like a teenager and we would tease him for it. My mother had grown up in a more traditional household where women did not speak, so she was quieter. Even now, when she laughs, it is more a kind of quiet shaking, which we call her 'silent mode'. My father's family is Pashtun, the largest ethnic group in Afghanistan and my mother is from the Arab ethnic minority. My mother was sixteen years old when she was married. My grandmother had been only thirteen, and her life had been extremely difficult. She was my grandfather's second wife and by the age of nineteen, when my grandfather died, she had seven children. She had to be both a mother and a father, whilst also finding work to support them all.

Girls are pushed into arranged marriages at very young ages out of fear. The honour of the family is hugely important and honour killings are commonplace, part of the culture of the country. An honour killing is the murder of a girl or woman who is perceived to have damaged the moral reputation – or honour – of the family. If a daughter goes astray, for example if she gets a boyfriend, leaves her home or deviates from her obligations in some way, then she has dishonoured the family and must be punished. That's why arranged marriages at an early age are so commonplace: the quicker a family can get rid of their daughter, by passing responsibility for her onto another man, the lower the risk of shame being brought on the family. So, even though my mother would probably have rather pursued her education, she was forced to wed my father – who she was loosely related to, since my maternal grandfather is the cousin of my paternal grandmother – to protect the honour of the family.

Despite coming from completely different worlds, my parents were forced into matrimony. It was a mutually beneficial arrangement for both sides of the families, because it meant that my coddled father would be forced to grow up and take on more responsibility and my mother would be one less mouth for her parents to feed. But the marital union took away my parents' choice and meant that they were shackled together for the rest of their lives. They were also expected to have children. In Afghan society, if a couple doesn't have children it is the woman who is blamed for the perceived failure, so my mother was forced down a path she may not have otherwise chosen for herself. Regardless, she brought me and my four younger brothers into the world.

There have always been more men in our family than women. I have four younger brothers: Shapoor, a year younger than me; Idris, two years younger; Tammim, four years younger; and Naveed, six years younger. My parents were determined to treat us fairly, to create an environment where all our voices would be heard. For even the simplest of decisions my father would call us all into the living room for a family meeting to discuss what we thought. Sometimes we would consider the most trivial of things, such as buying a new rug or TV for the house. I was almost frustrated by this: 'Why are you even bothering to ask us? Go buy it!' And my father would say: 'Hey, it's a decision for the family. Your opinion matters.'

I was the eldest, the first grandchild, the first kid in the family. I got a lot of attention and I liked it. I was often the only child among the adults. I grew used to being loud, opinionated and feeling heard. From a very young age, if there was a group of friends and family members that weren't listening or engaging with me, I would scream. I would amplify my voice as loud as I could so that they all paid attention to me. I wanted everybody in the room to be silent when I spoke. It sounds so spoilt and attention-seeking, but it was a direct result of the way I had been raised: to believe that what I said mattered, that I deserved to be seen and heard.

In my family there is a story that is often told from when I was four years old, when we were sheltering down in our basement. The fighting was at its worst and we were unable to buy food, but I demanded meat. My family gently explained to me that there was no way to get any. It was too dangerous outside. At that moment a black cat wound its way into the room. I pointed my little spindly finger at it and shouted: 'Go kill that black cat and bring me the meat.' My grandfather stood up and, despite the protestations and panicked pleas of other family members, climbed the stone stairs from the basement, made his way to the front door and peered across the yard before striding confidently but quietly towards our neighbour's house. Our neighbour owned a shop and my grandfather returned clutching a tin of meat. The joke is thus that I have always been a rebel and I have always got what I wanted.

My parents and grandparents also taught me to push back against injustice, to stick up and fight for myself, to make the world what I wanted it to be. If I went to them with a problem they would ask what I had done to solve it. Rather than give me definitive answers, they would mentor and coach me through my options. They wanted to help not by doing things for me but by nourishing my independence so I could rely on myself. This mindset and treatment – for the men of the household to value the opinions of women and encourage their autonomy – are not normal in our culture. My family were a tiny minority in thinking that way, and that was partly because they were not religious. Throughout my early childhood, it had felt as if we could ignore the world outside of our family bubble, but recently it had felt more and more difficult. I was used to running about with my brothers, but I was now at an age where more and more people were starting to have an opinion on what I was wearing and how I was behaving.

When the woman wearing the burqa was out of sight, I pulled my headscarf off and put it back in my bag. Shapoor shook his head. As we approached our courtyard, populated by apple, pear and pomegranate trees and beds of roses, the place I loved most in the world, our mother was standing in a beautiful light blue dress, waiting for us. She took one look at my sweaty, dust-stained face, my tangled hair, and pointed: 'Bath. Now.'

That night, I sat as a lace-like design was marked out on my hands with a wet mixture made of dried leaves, oil and water. My fingertips were sheathed, like they had been gently lowered into a muddy puddle. There was music playing behind the sound of women's laughter as they told each other stories. It was well known in my family that I had no interest in anything 'girly'. I preferred to play and compete with my brothers. When my grandfather proudly brought me a doll back from one of his trips abroad as a present, I shouted, 'Why don't they understand that I don't like dolls? Why do they keep bringing them to me?' before burning it in the fire pit outside.

I usually avoided being segregated in any way due to my gender, but that night there was something about the atmosphere, the soft flickering light, the sound of their carefree laughter and lack of self-consciousness (since they weren't in front of their husbands), the colours and patterns of the fabrics that felt magical to me. I sat waiting patiently for the henna to dry, then crack and be brushed away, leaving behind a deep burnt-orange-brown mandala effect on my skin. My mother turned my hands back and forth, inspecting them in the light. 'Beautiful,' she said, smiling, and I didn't even make a face.

She jerked her head towards a sudden sound of banging and loud voices outside. Suddenly the room was full of loud, confused voices.

'Hey, shut down the music. Stop everything,' said one of my aunt's husbands.

'The Taliban have taken control of the city. You need to leave, you need to get home right now.'

I looked at my mother, her face was pale. She took my hand as we found my grandmother. Panic took hold of the room around us as the women hurried about. The bride was taken away sobbing, her half-finished henna streaked down her arms.

'We need to get home now,' said my grandmother.

My mother nodded and hurried out of the room as my grandmother patted my hand and told me not to worry. My mother returned with bedsheets. She said all the phones had been disconnected. 'We can't walk about uncovered,' she said.

By this time it was the early hours of the morning. We walked by moonlight, swathed in sheets. I can't tell you how many kilometres we walked that night, the colour stripped from the world. It felt like we were the only people in the city as our shapeless figures trudged through the streets. Kabul was silent. I'd never seen it so quiet. Even the birds were hiding. It was as if the city was dead. Nobody spoke a word. I didn't dare open my mouth. I was scared that the sound of my dry lips parting would echo in the silence. I was scared by the expression on the faces of my mother and my grandmother. I realised I had never seen them terrified before. Only the swish of the bedsheets could be heard as we walked for what felt like hours, until we finally turned into our street. I heaved a sigh of relief – I hadn't even known where we were.

We stumbled through our front door and all of the family were in one room, waiting, shaking, petrified. My father and grandfather came and embraced us with relief, before quickly returning to the radio.

A voice announced that Mohammad Najibullah, the president of Afghanistan, was going to be castrated, tortured to death and hung from traffic-light poles outside the presidential palace, and the public was invited to watch. I saw my father and grandfather begin to cry, not for any love of Najibullah, but because they knew what was to come. Their tears took me by surprise. I had never seen either of them like that before. Broken. Despondent. Their tears spread around the room as relative after relative was overcome.

That night my mother, grandmother, brothers and I returned to the basement. For days we hid, desperate for news as the men tried to work out what was happening. The time that we had hidden in the basement before almost felt like a game compared to this time. The atmosphere was deadly. Palpable. There was fear and uncertainty. We were silent, flinching every time we heard voices or a truck in the street. After a couple of days, I plucked up the courage to ask my dad about my exams. It was the last term of the year. What was happening with our schools? Could I go back? How long would this last? How many days, weeks, months, years, this time? I asked about my classmates and friends. I didn't know where my friends lived, and I didn't have their phone numbers. Surely we would be allowed to say goodbye? Would the Taliban not even allow us that, the chance to go back and just exchange addresses? My father looked at me with sympathy as he sat down with me.

'The Taliban have announced there will be no school any more for girls. No study or work for women and girls. That all women must wear burqas.'

'But why? That doesn't make any sense,' I said.

'They see you as a threat', he said. 'Educated girls and women. You cannot be allowed.'

My dad made a bold choice and said that if his daughter couldn't go to school, neither would his sons. He didn't know what they would be taught in Taliban-influenced schools. My parents chose to keep their children together with the aim of finding a teacher to come to the house.

During the day, we would read our schoolbooks in the basement. Our parents would return, their faces drawn, and whisper to each other. Sometimes my mother would sob quietly. Her bright dresses had been replaced by dark, shapeless robes. After a couple of months, she decided she could not go outside any more.

All around us, the Taliban were recruiting and many people joined, not necessarily because they believed in Taliban ideology, but because they wanted to protect their families. The conversions tore up the culture of the city. Our neighbours were among those who joined. We had been so close with them, like family. We would bring our guests to their home and receive their guests at ours as if they were our own. The trust between neighbours had been high, and it had been the bedrock of our communities, but the Taliban ruptured that trust. Unity was dangerous to them. Suddenly, we could trust no one and it was impossible to discern friend from foe. Those who were recruited were desperate to prove themselves, to enforce Taliban rules and law to curry favour in an attempt to protect their own lives and the lives of their families. Previous loyalties became meaningless.

Many of my family members had served in the Afghanistan army or worked for the former government, which meant they were at extremely high risk, and the fact that we were not religious meant we were constantly questioned. By this point, my parents and grandparents had all lost their jobs. Salaries vanished and money was difficult to come by. My dad spent hours pounding the streets looking for odd jobs that would put a small amount on the table.

One night, he came home late. I could hear his voice, agitated and afraid. Dried blood was smeared across his face in a trail from his nose. His hair was grey, not from ageing but from dust that had been kicked up into it. He wasn't walking straight, and my mother and grandfather had to help him into a chair. They began cleaning his face with a cloth. He had been grabbed by a group of Taliban fighters and they had beaten him brutally. As he was kicked to the ground a friend of my uncle, who was nearby, had noticed what was going on and managed to create enough of a distraction for my dad to be able to wriggle free of his aggressors and run away, ducking down side streets and alleyways, into the darkness. He was lucky. At any moment he could have been hauled up, thrust onto the back of the pickup truck they were patrolling in and taken away, or beaten to death there and then.

Our house was no longer a safe place. It had shielded us from the bombings and airstrikes of the civil war, but the walls my grandfather had built could not withstand the sweeping sea of Taliban forces and allies invading every corner of the city. We had to get out. My uncle left first, ducking out into the night to reach a friend who knew people who could get us close to the border with Pakistan. While he was gone, we joined my parents in a treasure hunt, seeking out every important document or sentimental but identifying item. Trophies, certificates, photos, ID cards, anything and everything. We gathered them together in the middle of the room, a small mound of everything that identified our existence as individuals and a family, and then, striking a match, my grandfather set it all alight. It was a small fire, but the flames lashed around, sending a thick, dark cloud of smoke into the room. We could only release the smoke from the room gradually for fear of it being noticed outside. I stayed low, trying not to breathe in the fumes. A mixture of fear and nervous energy hung in the air, but as a child it felt exciting too, like the beginning of an adventure.

All we could take with us was a warm coat and one blanket each to protect us from the snow that had blanketed Kabul. 'Why am I not allowed to take that one? Why can't I take another? Why can't I say goodbye to my friends? We grew up together, we're friends! They always slept at our place!' Despite my increased understanding of what was going on, the situation was still very confusing.

Sometime between 4 and 5 a.m. we headed out into the dark winter's morning, towards the cars waiting for us a few blocks away. My shoes cut footprints into the snow, cushioning the sound of my steps but leaving a temporary marker of my existence.

The car was cold and we squeezed in as best we could. I gripped my blanket tight, flicking my feet at the hem to try and pull it around me. The tyres crunched in the snow as we pulled away. It was hard to see through the darkness, as the head- and tail-lights were turned off to mask our exit. We swapped cars twice, shunting from one to another, in daylight this time and far more conspicuously, but in more remote areas where we wouldn't be seen or heard.

We were aiming for Peshawar, the sixth-largest city in Pakistan and the closest city to the Afghanistan border. Over the days we were handed between smuggler groups like counterfeit goods. At the last stop before the border, the smugglers increased their price. We had no documentation because our identities put us at risk, and they knew it. My father and grandfather argued, but they had to be careful not to push back too much. We couldn't allow ourselves to be dumped in Afghanistan, so we gave them everything of value we had. At the border, we were left waiting for hours in caged queues, wondering whether our movers were as good as their word. I leant against my mum's legs, my blanket drooping from my hand. I was tired and hungry, standing in a maelstrom of noise, fear and desperation.

On the other side of the border, we were met by the next group of smugglers, who took us to a dilapidated farm where we spent the night in a stinking barn with cows. It had taken two days for us to reach our destination, and we hadn't eaten a single thing in that time. We arrived in pitch darkness, shivering and stinking of manure. In the dim light cast by hundreds of tiny fires there were dark shapes. Tents stretching as far as I could see.

2

Football is about choices. When to run, when to pass. Control and release. When you play in a team, you are part of the smallest unit of society. The eleven of you making choices that come together in an expression of all of you. The team is you and you are the team. But it begins with the ball and you. You and the ball. Open your eyes.

Dust. Dust and heat. A jumble of dirty canvases stretching all the way to the horizon. Squat, irregular buildings built from the local mud bricks are jotted here and there. Everything is stained by the dust. Plastic bottles and rubbish cover the ground. Ashes from the fires pollute the air. All around us are the sounds of a hundred thousand people talking, shouting, moaning. And babies. Babies crying.

That first morning in the refugee camp, pain and hunger stirred me awake as the sun rose. My whole body ached. My shoulder felt bruised from the pressure of one of my brother's knees pressing against it. We shifted about, trying to find a comfortable position in the broken-down tent we had found the night before in the darkness. That morning, our parents had gone to try and find us somewhere to stay. When they returned, they took us to a house, of sorts. They had used almost everything we had left to get it. The walls were made from local mud – thick, dark and heavy, a cool haven from the oppressive heat. We had two small rooms between eleven of us and a front door that could be locked, though anyone with a bit of strength could breach it. 'Stay here,' said my dad. 'Don't open the door to anyone but us.'

My parents, grandparents, aunt and uncle left again. They went to speak to representatives of the UNHCR (United Nations High Commissioner for Refugees). They searched for work, for food and places where we could get water. They filtered through the camp, mapping out our new surroundings, the lessons from my father's military school and army upbringing kicking into action. They returned by nightfall and discussed what they had learnt. They worked as a team. The attitude was to take action, fight, stay together as a unit and never give up. We learnt that there was a whole city in the camp, including shops, schools and hospitals. That first night in the mud house, I lay on my father's chest, listening to his heartbeat until I finally slept.

My dad found some work in construction, lugging huge containers of cement on his back. He had worked in an office for his entire career after leaving military school, so this type of work was new to him, but he was determined to do whatever he could to support us, regardless of the physical toll it took on his body. He would return home with his muscles seized up and my mum would spend the evening pushing the base of her hands into the grooves around his shoulder blades in an attempt to ease the aching pain. My grandfather managed to secure a small advance, which allowed him to buy some food and scraps of old canvas to cover the dirt floor. We didn't have any spare clothes – we had left everything behind – so we didn't wash or change. Eventually the smell and dirt became normal, until it reached the point where it could get no worse. I no longer remembered what clean smelt like.

We had just enough to survive, living on one small meal of bread a day, which was often stale and had to be steamed back to life with water. Sometimes we would be able to get a small helping of rice or lentils in one of the UNHCR buildings. I knew we had lost everything, I knew I couldn't be fussy, and I knew I had to take on the role of being a second mother to my brothers and cousins whilst the adults in the family tried their best to find work. Sometimes they would spend hours searching, only to come back empty-handed.

My dad registered us in a UNHCR-supported school in the camp. I would lead my brothers along the dusty paths, weaving in and out through the maze of tents and buildings. As soon as the sun came up, the ground would shimmer from the heat. The school allowed us to make new friends and meet new people, and they were all Afghans, which helped us settle in. We would stay at school until the afternoon, and we were given notebooks by the UNHCR. They had a blue cover with the UNHCR and UNICEF logo across the front, and even though they weren't clean or new-smelling like my schoolbooks back home, I treasured them. I refused to miss a minute of school, not because I enjoyed it but because I had been raised to value education. I didn't want to be absent even for one day; I had already missed two years.

Sometimes, if my mother wasn't home, if she was working or running late, I would take my youngest brother, Naveed, with me to school. I would take a cloth to his face and scrub it clean before dressing him in the smartest clothes I could find. We didn't have a baby carrier or a buggy so I would lift his toddler weight upon my skinny arms and waddle down the dusty road. He would sit next to me in class, happily chomping on grapes and an apple without any fuss. Everybody liked him. It helped that he was very cute, so it became acceptable for him to be there even though it was exceptional. I didn't resent taking him with me because I didn't know any other way of doing things. I felt like a sheep dog, constantly steering my siblings and cousins back into the immediate orbit of our home or shepherding them to and from school. But we all helped each other in our family. That's just the way it was.

When school had finished and I'd dropped my brothers off at home, I would snake stealthily back through the camp to find my grandfather, to help him with whatever work he had picked up. He would make bricks by hand, stuffing mud into a little wooden frame to shape them, before clunking them out onto the ground to dry out in the sun. Those handmade bricks were used to build houses in the camp, not dissimilar to ours, although the bricks used for ours had not been made with the precision of my grandfather's hand. He would turn out between a hundred and two hundred bricks a day, and each would be as close to perfect as the rudimentary tools would allow. I helped by bringing him water to moisten the mud enough to allow it to be forced into its new shape. I felt useful. I liked the way the bricks would stutter out of the frame like pieces of a sandcastle, and I loved the company of my grandfather. He would tell me stories of his travels, describing the great cities he had visited in Europe and Russia, and I would listen, imagining these magical places beyond the dust and the tents.

The camp was disorganised and chaotic. It was a lawless city. What little order there was came from an unofficial leader who was a conservative Pashtun, as were most of the Taliban from whom we had fled. In the camp there was the expectation that women and girls should cover their faces, so that only their eyes were visible, but you could do that with a scarf; you didn't need a burqa. One afternoon, I just couldn't take the heat any longer and I lowered my scarf a little. I just wanted to breathe. I thought I was alone, but a rickshaw driver on the other side of the road saw. He swung back towards me and drove into me with his rickshaw. I was stunned. I had been clutching a stack of books, which flew into the air, and I was thrown to the ground by the force of the impact. My clothes were ripped from landing on the stony ground, and I started crying from the shock and pain. That night, my mum cleaned the dirt from my bruised body, black and blue, with tears in her eyes. 'Please, try and wear your scarf,' she said.

I made friends with several girls of a similar age to me, including a girl named Kamila, who I met at the school. She was kind, funny and quiet. Most of her family had disappeared or been killed; only one male relative remained in the family by the time everyone fled to Pakistan in search of a safer environment for the women. Kamila and I were very different, but we were bonded by our similar circumstances and a mutual understanding of our world at that moment in time. Kamila struggled in English class. When the teacher told her to read passages out loud I would whisper the words to her if she got stuck, and sometimes I would tease her afterwards, whispering silly things that I knew would make her laugh. Friendship is essential during times of hardship, and small moments of fun and laughter can be the only remedy to help you through.

The camp hummed with danger. Arguments and fights broke out over food and water. There were harsh punishments for stealing. Children went missing, and the sound of a mother wailing when one disappeared ricocheted through the gaps between the tents. There was a rumour that kids were sliced open, and clumsily – often catastrophically – sewn back up after their kidneys had been stolen to be sold.

One morning, trudging around the edge of camp on my way to school, I stopped, frozen and terrified. I had to force myself to unfreeze, to turn my brothers away and distract them from what was taking place. I tried to keep my eyes on the ground as I shuffled my brothers past, but I kept snatching glances at the scene before us. I couldn't help it. I couldn't not watch what was going on, but I was also trying to stay on guard, to check we hadn't caught anyone's attention.

A boy, a year or two younger than me and a similar age to my younger brothers, about ten years old, was lying face down in the dirt, tear-stained and lifeless, unable to scream, as a man whipped him with a piece of frayed rope before he began to lurch and move over him, groaning as he did so. I didn't have the vocabulary to articulate what was happening to the boy, but I knew it was wrong. It was sucking his soul from his body. I could see that in his eyes. This was how I learnt what rape is. Back at home, I asked my mum about what I had seen. She looked broken, relieved and despairing all at once. She explained that what we had witnessed was rape and that we had to be extremely careful as the camp was not safe.

I had to grow up quickly. Quicker than I wanted to, than my family wanted me to, and quicker than I should have had to. I would try to pass through the camp like a shadow, unnoticed, gripped by a fear and a tightness in my chest that kept me hypervigilant. We weren't allowed to visit friends or go to other people's houses or tents. My parents taught us how to be streetwise, to be wary of everyone. They taught us how to survive.

I plotted the safest routes when I went anywhere. I watched everyone like a hawk, taking note of people's movements, their eyes, their hands. I quickly became desensitised to the most horrific violence because it was safer to ignore, move confidently and quietly, and escape the scenes, rather than freeze and show fear or weakness. I paid closer attention to what was going on and I stored up questions to be asked later. My grandfather always tolerated my questions better than anyone else. He would explain why people were behaving the way they were, what their motivations were – jealousy, pride or fear. I began to think about the world in a different way, to be cautious and to anticipate the outcomes of situations.

Gradually, my family found their feet. They hustled relentlessly for work and eventually my mum got a job as a teacher. My dad managed to save enough money to set up a little store, a small supermarket, in the camp, which he ran with my aunt. We slowly shifted from surviving to thriving, and it was because of teamwork that the family was so strong. We stayed together as a unit, with every member of the team contributing. Having previously been a wealthy man, my grandfather was quite well known, but he stayed humble. We all did. We didn't dwell on the things we had lost. We just worked hard to improve our conditions.

As life shuttled between school and home, my parents returning late and exhausted, my father telling us stories of his day and my mother laughing quietly, four years passed. In that time, I began to form a new identity. My brothers and I would play cricket and football in the dust. I found that when we played sports, I could tune out our environment. It offered us a brief escape. I started thinking of Pakistan as our country, our home. For me, Afghanistan was gone for good. We didn't have access to news from Afghanistan any more and it felt more and more distant. My youngest brothers, Tammim and Naveed, couldn't remember anything before the camp, and Naveed had learnt to talk there. The image of Afghanistan that remained planted in my mind, from the day we left, was of the bright, white snow. It never snowed in Pakistan, so snow symbolised Afghanistan for me. It gave me a cosy feeling, of a home I had pretty much forgotten.

As a family, we began to plan our way out of the camp. There was no process for leaving, no registration required – you just moved as soon as you could afford to. My dad's store had grown from a little shop into a supermarket where he employed the men of the family, and the women, including my mum, worked as teachers. We were able to rent an apartment in Peshawar in an area populated mainly with families who had left Afghanistan. I had entered the camp when I was nine years old; I left when I was thirteen.

Our apartment had a television. We watched all the Bollywood films and TV series we could, we watched as many light entertainment shows as possible, and we watched sport. So much sport. Now that I could watch *and* play cricket I started to understand the game better. I started to watch football too. It was a very different game to cricket and it appealed to me.

In our new neighbourhood, I was able to join in street football games, huge games with uneven teams. I loved it. We ran after the ball in packs, laughing until we couldn't breathe. Once again, it felt as if I could be free. Dress and behaviour codes for girls were much less strict on the streets of Peshawar than they had been in the camp. I made friends with classmates, most of whom had left Afghanistan more or less the same time as our family and had grown up in Pakistan, and we would go shopping in the evenings, since the shops stayed open late. We were free of the constant danger of the camp, and during the two years that we lived in Peshawar we began to open ourselves up to the world and to new experiences, like flowers. We stopped thinking about the past and began thinking about the future. Until the news interrupted our lives, again.

My brothers and I had had been lounging on the sofa in our apartment, watching a Bollywood film, when my father came running in. 'Quick,' he shouted, 'switch to the news.'

We groaned. There was a banner across the bottom of the screen with the words 'War in Afghanistan'. We looked on as the US set fire to the country we hadn't seen in years. Only a month before, we had watched the constant replaying of footage showing the planes hitting the Twin Towers in New York. Seeing the footage now, we didn't know how to feel. The Taliban had forced our family from our home and threatened our lives, so we wanted to celebrate anything that hurt them. But so many relatives and friends remained in the country. They were losing their homes and lives to the bombings. I watched my parents flinch with every blast, feeling the destruction of everything they once knew. We didn't know what was happening to ordinary people back in our neighbourhood in Khair Khana. We didn't know if our house still stood.

After we had lived for months with war as background noise to daily life, in December 2001 the Taliban were forced from power and it was announced to the world that a new government would be formed. There were calls for those who had previously fled the country to return home.

My father and grandfather were fizzing with excitement. A part of them that had been cut off was suddenly returned, as if blood was again flooding through into their bodies, or colour returning to a black-and-white world. There were tears. Lots of tears. It was a bittersweet moment. In their minds, there had never been any doubt that they would go back, but they had spent six years building a life that suddenly meant nothing to them. For them Pakistan had been an unfortunate sidestep, an enforced one, a hated one. There was never any consideration for what would have to be left behind. Their bodies were in Pakistan, but their amputated hearts and ambitions had never left Kabul. They were always operating in limbo, waiting and hoping to return.

The plan was that my father and uncle would travel back home first, to fix up what remained of the house as best they could, while my grandfather would stay with us for two months so we could finish the school term and sit our exams. My father abandoned everything at the drop of a hat, not even bothering to sell stock off cheaply. Instead, he gave it all away to speed up the process; the financial loss was irrelevant to him. He climbed into our car one morning with my uncle and they headed for the border, crossing in very different circumstances to the reverse journey.

I cried and protested. I couldn't help it. I tried to resist the attempts to shift us back to Kabul, but nobody would listen. I felt hugely conflicted, caught between my own raging emotions and the new light I could see gleaming from my parents and grandparents. Peshawar had already started to empty out. We were rattling around, and after our exams were over half my class vanished overnight. Like our family, other families left everything too. Nobody of my father's and grandfather's generations cared about the lives they had built in Pakistan. Everyone swept out of the country at a pace which meant there was no time to spare for saying goodbye to friends, no tying up of loose ends. The delicate ecosystem we had lived in collapsed, rapidly. Every week, a new friend left. Once again, I felt like I was losing my friends, my identity and my community.

'You always say you want to involve us in decisions,' I shouted to my father before he left. 'But this, this is the biggest decision and you're the only one making it!'

'It is our country,' he said calmly. 'It is where we belong. Pakistan is not our country, Pakistan is not our home. This is somewhere we tried to survive. Now it is time to go home.'

My brothers and I raged at the unfairness of it. My mother calmly told us that one day we would understand. But we argued back, telling her that we didn't have friends there any more, we didn't have a network or a community, we had no idea what the impact of Taliban rule and the subsequent invasion would have had on the streets of Khair Khana. I had left Afghanistan when I was nine, a child. I was now fifteen years old and the idea of leaving everything I knew filled me with anger, which I forced myself to suppress each time I witnessed the joy emanating from my parents and grandparents. We recognised their delight, but we could not relate to it.

When we travelled back to Afghanistan, the roads were rammed with cars and buses full of people. As we drove into Kabul it was hard not to stare. Half-destroyed buildings, like broken teeth in a mouth. Trees stripped of leaves, bare. Burnt-out cars at the side of the road. Everything was coated in dust. The place was desolate. All I could think about were the people who were missing from every destroyed building, trying to imagine who they were. We could sense the fear. The palpable euphoria of the returning masses shifted into shock and despair. Tears slid down my cheeks as I stared at the rubble of a destroyed city, trying to see something I recognised, trying to see some remnants of the place we once called home.

3

To play a game with your hands, to throw and to catch, is to use skills that have evolved throughout the history of humanity. But to kick a ball is to learn a skill almost entirely for the purpose of play. Open your eyes.

'Hey! Hey, you!'

I glanced across the road to the man who was looking at me and pointing. I realised my scarf had come loose. I panicked. I had been walking home from the local shop when a ball came rolling towards me so I had put my shopping bags down to kick it back. I flicked it up into the air, unable to resist. I had tucked my hair back into my scarf quickly, but it slipped.

'Hey, how old are you?' He started to walk quickly towards me.

I walked in the other direction, ignoring him, back towards the shops, into the crowd of people where I thought I would be safe. Suddenly there were people all around me. A pickup truck full of men with guns stopped right beside me. I froze. One of them, a man with a large turban and long beard was looking at me, his eyes tearing me apart. I was a teenager so I didn't need to wear a burqa, just a scarf, but clearly that was wrong in his eyes. Before I could think, a nearby shopkeeper grabbed me by the hand and pulled me into a house by his shop. He shouted, 'Oh, please, don't mind her, she's just my daughter.'

They turned their attention towards him, knocking him to the ground, kicking and hitting him. He cowered, blood spattering onto the dust from his bottom lip.

'You let your daughter dress like this?'

In the chaos, I managed to slip away and hurried towards my house. My heart was pounding in my chest. It was not the first time since we returned to Kabul that I felt like I wanted to cry.

It had become a city of ghosts and shadows. Whole walls of buildings were either gone, or riddled with bullet holes. Everything felt dark, ancient and broken. War had drained life from the city, leaving a grey, rotting corpse behind. Even the trees were dry and limp. Nothing felt beautiful. Though their influence had lessened since the invasion by the US in 2001, the Taliban's legacy was everywhere. TVs were smashed and VHS cassettes hung from power lines by the ribbons torn from within them, to remind people that these things were no longer allowed. There was no music, other than the ultra-religious chants praising Taliban laws and commemorating fighters killed in battle. They pressured people to be pious and conform. Fear gripped the city. People felt forced to go to mosques and pray.

Women had to wear burqas. Everyone looked the same, engulfed by big blue burqas, eyes hidden behind mesh or laced panels. Women were beaten for wearing sandals. They were even beaten just for being outside. You would hear the women screaming and children crying before you saw them. Taliban adherents beat women and children alike, leaving them lying on the ground. Men were struck down and carted away in the backs of cars, never to be seen again. We had no idea who we could trust in the neighbourhood. Some of our neighbours had disappeared, and those who remained hid away in their houses. It was like we had left the freedom of a lush garden in Peshawar to return to a cage. Everywhere I went, I was watched. It was worse than the refugee camp.

At school, I was put into the correct class for my age, but there were older women in there too, ones that had been in that class prior to the Taliban taking control. They hadn't been allowed to go to school after that, since women were banned from education. I was fifteen years old, in a class with women who were twenty or twenty-one. Women who now had children of their own, who had been forced to get married, the only role they were deemed worthy of in Taliban society – and, even then, not that worthy. There were huge differences between us as a result. They whispered behind my back. They said I was a slut and called me unclean. Every time I answered a question in class, I felt their eyes boring into me. I could sense their resentment and I couldn't blame them.

We had heard stories of what it had been like to live under the Taliban, but I was one of the few who had got away. As a woman the only way to survive was to be seen to be pious, to conform and to subsequently police the behaviour of other women. Even though the Taliban were officially gone from power, their methods and worldview were not. The women in my class, and those who behaved similarly in the rest of society, were driven by a fear of the Taliban's return. A fear that I didn't share as urgently as they did. Though we were all officially allowed to wear school uniform, many of them still wore a burqa. And because I did not, I would be stopped in the corridors and streets on the way to and from school. 'Where is your family, how can they let you dress like this? Are you even a Muslim?' Schoolteachers too picked on those of us who had returned. They made us feel like we had done something wrong in fleeing; they treated us like we were criminals.

I was still angry that my family were stopping me from doing what I wanted, and I didn't feel happy at school. I was desperate for change. My parents and grandparents had returned to Afghanistan filled with so much hope, but mine was draining away. We had relatives who had stayed hidden and survived. They did what they needed to do to get by and they were now rapt for new experiences, for stories of life in Pakistan, for culture, for the smallest things that I had taken for granted. They were desperate to watch a Bollywood movie. TVs, videos, cassettes, and other technology had been banned under the Taliban and the fear of being caught with something like this even after they had fallen was still strong.

Relatives who had taken shelter in our dilapidated house had hidden a VHS player and a TV in a hole in the backyard, so we smuggled them both inside. We managed to get an old Bollywood film on the black market and, for special occasions, we would go down to the basement, with a blanket covering the one small window in the room to hide what we were doing, and dampen the sound. We would gather around our little makeshift cinema, keeping the volume so low that everyone had to be completely silent to hear the music. That was our only entertainment, our only joy. Once again, we found ourselves in the place where we had sheltered from bombs and fighting, hiding from the outside world, but this time we were hiding from an enemy that lived in the minds of people around us.

Because my family weren't religious, we were automatically distrusted and regarded with suspicion. My reluctance to wear a burqa, and my habit of walking around in just a headscarf, cast a shadow onto the male members of my family. People thought it was dishonourable. I was called terrible names, all of the time, and every one of them had to endure it too. My brothers, Tammim and Naveed, were still children, yet they also had to witness the verbal abuse of their sister.

One day, when I was walking home, someone called my name. It was my brother, Shapoor. 'Khalida, where have you been? Mum and Dad sent me to find you.' His voice was stern but his face softened when I turned around.

'What happened?' he asked me.

'Nothing, it's fine. What's it got to do with you? Since when did you start controlling what I do?'

'You know I don't. But I can't spend my entire life arguing with the whole neighbourhood about you.'

His face was tight, his jaw clenched. He looked much older than fourteen. I could still see a faint bruise on his face which had appeared a couple of days ago. Though he refused to explain where it had come from, I knew that it was because of what the boys in his class were saying about me, the names they were calling me. In a gentler voice, he said, 'Please, just tie your scarf and wear loose clothes so your body isn't visible when you're out here. You just can't run around here like *that*.' He gestured towards me, taking in my dishevelled scarf and my hair, but also my body, which had suddenly started to betray me with bumps and curves that I couldn't control. 'They're already suspicious of us.'

Later that afternoon, I was kicking a ball against the wall in our courtyard. Watching the different ways it bounced back as I used different parts of my foot, trying to stop it dead as it returned to me the way I had seen others do when they played. My father came outside and watched me.

'Khalida, I need to talk to you.'

'One second,' I said.

'Now, please!' There was a sharpness to his voice. Not anger, as he was hardly ever angry with us. But something. An edge. 'I have been speaking with your brothers and your mother. We all agree it is not safe for you to walk around in the street.'

I looked at him with a flash of anger I was unable to hide. He was expecting it. If he had been angry, tried to lay down the law, I would have fought back. But there was no anger, no righteous discipline. Only sadness and worry. He sighed.

'Perhaps it is our fault. We wanted you to grow up strong, to believe that your voice matters, because it does matter. But it is different out there.' He trailed off, gestured beyond the walls, taking in the whole of the city, the country. 'I am not saying forever,' he said. 'I believe that things will get better. But you must let them move at their own speed. Right now, it is too dangerous. And not just for you.' I thought of my younger brothers, of the bruises on their faces.

'Khalida?' My father was looking at me, as if he had asked me a question. 'Will you promise me? Promise you won't play football out in the streets any more?'

I thought of how my family had reacted when they arrived at the refugee camp. They hadn't shouted or sulked. They had got on with finding a way.

I nodded slowly.

As I stood in the dappled shade of our family courtyard, it hit me that I would never again have the freedoms of a child in Afghanistan. If I was going to find a way through this situation it would be as a woman. But I was equally certain that I would find a way, whatever it took.

4

The language of football is the language of war. Your coach is the general and you are the soldiers. Strategy and shots. Defence and attack. You need to win your battles. The national anthem plays and the crowd sheds patriotic tears. But it is also a game. In this tension between conflict and play, destruction and creation, there is something essentially human. Something beautiful. Open your eyes.

'Whores,' the man hissed.

The men called out insults to our families for letting us play football, snatching up our bags and tipping them upside down, sending schoolbooks flying into the air and tumbling to the ground. They kicked our goalposts made of stones disdainfully away and painstakingly scuffed our pitch lines into obscurity in the dust. The ringleader grabbed a scarf that lay on the floor and shoved it hard into the face of one of the players, sending her stumbling backwards. Then, silent and seething, somehow more terrifying than he was before, he strode into the centre of the yard, a mixture of rage and pleasure in his expression. Revealing a large knife that he held up in front of us dramatically, he proceeded to stab into our football: once, twice, a third time. Then he threw it to the ground. It was a performance, like a magician putting on a show, but it was also a very real threat.

To be a young woman in Afghanistan is to grow up with violence. To learn not to fight back. To fight back is to risk being killed. If you are beaten it's because you were at fault, you must have done something wrong. There were twenty of us in the yard that day, far more of us than of them, but there was nothing we could do, because we knew the consequences. Our crime? Kicking a ball, playing sport, having fun.

We watched as the object that allowed us an escape for an hour a day lay crumpled on the floor. The man walked back to his friends and they all laughed, looking over at us, spitting on the ground before they climbed back over the wall. When they were gone, a feeling of relief rippled through the group. The ten of us exhaled at the same time.

'I told you this would happen,' said one of the girls, shaking her head. Another stifled a sob.

This had all started with me kicking a ball in the schoolyard. My mum had got a job teaching physical education in my school, but the expectations of physical education in an Afghan school are very far removed from the Western idea of PE. Instead of engaging in sports, we were expected to use that time to cook or sew. My mum tried to teach us a few recipes, but she was not a great cook and so she started to look for other fun things for us to do in that time. Eventually, she was given access to some sports equipment. There wasn't a huge amount, but there were a few footballs and basketballs.

Our school was surrounded by tall concrete walls, which were both oppressive and freeing. They protected us girls from prying eyes and allowed the public to ignore our existence. While I waited for my mum to finish teaching, I would help myself to a ball and kick it around the yard. We didn't have any courts or pitches, just the hard stones. I would try and stay quiet to avoid drawing attention to myself, so I didn't kick the ball against the walls, but I would dribble it around and this allowed me to escape mentally. That is how my football journey really started.

Some of the girls in the younger classes saw me. They watched and chatted, moved on, and occasionally spoke to me. One day I was dribbling the ball around, imagining the players

I was beating falling into the dust around me, when I felt someone watching. She was a couple of years younger than me, but already slightly taller, with short hair. I dribbled the ball over to her.

'I'm Khalida,' I said.

'You need to use your other foot more,' she said, frowning slightly.

'OK, coach,' I said, smiling. 'What should I call you?'

'I'm Samira,' she said.

And then, we were two. A tiny team.

Samira's story was like mine. Her love of sport was forged outside the oppressive culture of Afghanistan. In Iran she had played football with her brothers and found a sense of freedom in it. She was good, far better than me. She started to teach me the game properly. Before meeting her, all I had known was how to chase the ball. There was little else I could do; I didn't have any talent or skills. I just ran and kicked, intuitively following the ball rather than actively controlling it. Her personality was very different to mine: she was thoughtful and much quieter. I would run around clowning, trying to make her smile, and she would look at me, slightly puzzled, as if I was a dog riding a bicycle.

She expanded my understanding of what I could do and as we played, others watched. She understood how the game worked, she could picture how to get the ball to another player. I would laugh when she did something incredible and she would shrug afterwards as if it was nothing. We had fun, and we could tell that people were taking an interest. So many girls had forgotten what fun looked like, and we were enjoying ourselves. Some would stand and watch, clearly wanting to join in. So we would go and ask them to play. Many didn't, walking away shyly. But some did.

Then we started approaching girls and expanding our ranks. We committed to getting to school early to play before classes began. School began at 7 a.m. and so we aimed to get in at 5 or 6 a.m. It was so liberating. We wore our school uniforms, we didn't change and we didn't care if we smelt afterwards. I would take in wet wipes and some perfume (which was banned), so the smell wasn't too bad. I sweated a lot and I was *very* self-conscious of it, but I wasn't going to let that stop me.

Once we had been doing the early mornings for a while, we switched to playing in the afternoon. Schools were so overwhelmed by the many women wanting to re-attend and take back the years of education they had missed that the school day was split in two. Some were given sessions in the morning and others in the afternoon. My classes were in the morning, so I was finished by early afternoon. There was a crucial one-hour gap between us finishing school and the next half-day beginning. In that time, the only people around were cleaners and caretakers, and they didn't care what we got up to.

I always had a good relationship with the cleaners and other school staff, because during breaks I would help clean. I would wipe down desks and grab a broom, joining in with the Sisyphean attempts to contain the relentless dust. I helped the cleaners because they were there to help us and it felt like the right thing to do. I would smuggle in a larger-than-average lunch to share and bring in unwanted clothes for them and their children. I got to know them all. We would laugh together and I felt loved; they would refer to me as their daughter. I spent time with them in the same way I hung around my father and grandfather, chipping into adult conversations and listening to their stories. I didn't want anything in return – that was never the objective – but they overlooked us playing football anyway. They just let us get on with it. They knew I was in charge, that I was the ringleader, but they let us play uninterrupted. So, we played in that small one-hour window between the two school days.

With the school quiet, we could be ourselves, we could talk, and we could also celebrate, shout and express ourselves playing football. These were new experiences and new emotions. Girls shrieking with glee at having wrongfooted the goalkeeper, before lashing the ball between the rock-goalposts against the wall, which we imagined would ripple like a net – this was not normal or accepted. Shouting for my teammate to pass me the ball or gasping loudly as my leg entwined with another's, seeking to grapple the ball free of their possession, was utterly exhilarating. These girls had spent their lives being taught that women were to exist in the shadows, on the periphery. Quiet and unassuming. Since returning to the city, I had felt the weight of this expectation crushing down on me, but every day during this time I felt able to be myself.

I organised the players around me and together our voices became louder. We embraced being vocal, brash and playful, and our eyes were opened to new emotional heights we didn't realise were possible. On the football pitch we were in charge for the first time. We made decisions. Should I pass the ball? Should I take a shot? Should I move into this space? Should I dive left or right to try and make a save? We had control. We were laser-focused. And we lapped up the opportunity to think independently.

After a few months, we had enough girls to make up two teams that could play against each other, which transformed the game for us. We would chuck down our school bags and play, the material of our hijabs catching in the wind as we ran, laughter ringing round the yard. Some girls played on the stony ground without shoes on. Others had shoes that were so ill-fitting and unsuited to football that if they kicked the ball their shoe would fly into the air with it, sending us all into hysterics. It was liberating, and so much fun.

Many young women joined us, of all different ages. We hid what we were doing from the principal and the teachers. We knew that they would be resistant to our activities, since it was risky for them to permit it. They were focused on shaping us into the traditional image of young womanhood: women were expected to be calm, timid and quiet, to stay home and clean, to live a life of service and to eventually bear children for their husbands. Deviating from this in any way was severely frowned upon, so we stood out as troublemakers. We began to gain reputations for having bad manners and for being brought up in the wrong way.

One evening, my mum came to my room. 'Khalida, there is a rumour you are playing football at school.'

'It's not a rumour,' I said. 'We are. There are lots of us. We love it.' I was embarrassed to find that there were tears in my eyes. My mother nodded and touched my face.

From that point on, she did what she could to enable us. She wanted to give us the opportunity to continue and to expand, and she took great risks by doing so. I sensed that she was living vicariously through us, in a way. Her dreams had been taken away from her at a young age when she was forced to marry, and so in her view she would do everything she could to make sure that us girls had opportunities she didn't have. She wanted us to access the things we were interested in and passionate about, whatever that might be. In our case it was football. She lived through our smiles and energy, through our belief that we could push back against society's expectations of us and that things could be different.

We got more audacious in our recruitment techniques. We would duck into classes, taking advantage of the two or three minutes between teachers changing over to pitch to the class. Full of energy, I would stand at the front of the class and say: 'Hey, we play football at this time, you can come and join if you like. Come and join. We will play football, play sports and have some fun.' We got people excited about being part of a small rebellion.

I became known as the crazy football girl in school, but at the same time I was working extra hard in my classes to make sure that there was no excuse to end the extracurricular activity. I didn't want my parents to see football as a barrier to my education. I felt the pressure to excel in every subject to make sure that I didn't lose football. It was the only happiness my teammates and I had. What had been my escape became their escape too. A small place, a bubble in the world, where we reclaimed our lost childhoods, where the predetermined futures mapped out before us, based solely on our sex, dissipated temporarily. Football allowed us to feel free. It was like magic.

There was a problem though: the noise of our voices, the shouts and sighs of our newly discovered passion carried beyond the concrete walls. We didn't realise that people were listening on the other side. The walls made us feel like the outside world didn't exist, but it did. People had started to pay attention on the other side, wondering what we were doing and why we were still in school in the midday heat. They were curious, confused by the sounds. And so, our sanctuary was breached.

We did take precautions; we made new rules to try and avoid attention. We played silent football. We decided we could have no screaming, no shouting, no celebrating, nothing. Silence. If we stayed quiet, hopefully whoever was lurking on the other side of the wall would lose interest. Silent football is unrealistic, though. You cannot control your emotions during a game. It's natural to express joy, pain, frustration, disappointment. It's instinctive, and we failed to contain ourselves.

The day when a body swung over the top and thudded down into the yard, then another, and another, and another, until there were five men looking curiously at our makeshift pitch, punctured our joy with the reminder that we were not free. The attack illustrated to me just how powerful football could be. It was more than a game, and it could be used as a tool for pushing back against what they told us we could be.

Before they left, they walked around mockingly, like zombies, arms outstretched, legs straight with a stuttering gait. They said women couldn't walk properly as they staggered sardonically through our safe space. 'Women walk like this. How can they play football? Football is for men. It's a man's game. It's not for women. Go wash the dishes. Clean the house. Go give birth.'

I felt like if we stopped playing football, we would be letting them win. We would be accepting defeat. This would impact how we saw ourselves: instead of strong, autonomous individuals we would be victims. We would come to see ourselves as inferior, the way they wanted us to feel. But what they said didn't make sense – it was nonsense – and it made me question how deep the problems in our society and in our country were. These men had come into my space, my safe zone, near my home, into my school, in my community, in *my* country, and tried to stop me from being me. No. I would not acquiesce. They would not win.

I didn't have any answers to this new problem and how to navigate it, but I knew that giving up wasn't an option at all. I knew there were always two choices – to take action or give up – and I would fight tooth and nail rather than down tools. The day after the men climbed the wall, I turned up at our usual time, only to find fewer than half of the girls there.

'Where is everyone?' I said to Samira.

'Isn't it obvious?' she said.

Across the yard, I saw a girl who normally played with us walking quickly in the opposite direction with her head down.

'Hey! Where are you going?' I caught up with her. 'Hey,' I said more gently. 'You can't let them win.'

'We're not all lucky like you, Khalida,' she said wearily. 'My father will beat me half to death if he finds out about this. Then he'll stop me coming to school at all.'

'But you're so good,' I said. She looked at me with something like pity.

'That doesn't matter,' she whispered. Then she carried on walking.

I was very aware that I came from different circumstances to almost all the other girls. Like them, when I was out in the world, others made decisions on my behalf. I couldn't wear my hair short or walk the streets without my headscarf, otherwise I would be judged. Everything about my appearance and behaviour was judged by society, and I had to act accordingly for my own safety. Likewise, at school, I had little choice and zero control. Teachers controlled what I could do and say. I was unable to push back, even in the most respectful way, without being treated as insolent and a troublemaker. But when I got home and shut the door to the world outside, I had a supportive family who were on my side. A father and brothers who were not like the man with the knife, who would defend me against them. Most of the other girls went home to men who were like that man.

I was so angry and frustrated. These men, with their knives, their power and their violence, had taken away the one thing that made us happy. They killed a small hope that had been growing among us. After we had finished playing a three-a-side game one day, Samira and I lay with our heads on a goalpost.

'This isn't working,' I said. 'We need more players.'

'Well, who?' said Samira. 'We've already gone around the whole school. And most of the ones who said yes are now terrified that men are going to come climbing over the wall again. Face it: they're not coming back.'

I sat up. 'Then we need to find other schools.'

5

You don't need to think. Pass. Run. Shoot. To play is to disappear into something bigger than yourself, to be aware of yourself not as an individual but as something else. The messiness, the noise of life fades away until it is you and the team and the ball. Open your eyes.

'As I say, we would be very happy to sponsor you,' said Muhammad Anwar Jigdalek, the president of the NOC, the National Olympic Committee of Afghanistan, grasping my hand in his. He was watching me closely, his eyes analytical, but the way he was looking at me was somehow unsettling. He was a large man with a trimmed grey beard and as he reclined back in his chair the hydraulics squeaked in protest. I glanced at my mother, who was sitting to one side. I could tell she was furious.

I tried, one last time, to tell him I wasn't looking for sponsorship for myself. We wanted the school teams we had created to be formally recognised in leagues, to be able to compete in them, and we wanted to found a women's national football team. We needed equipment and support. But again, he acted as if I was being cute, as if he and I were flirting. This is a pattern of behaviour that many men in Afghanistan often deploy. They pretend they are taking you seriously, humour you, dangle the carrot of being heard in front of you, but they are only interested – temporarily – in attention. It is all about control. I glanced at the two other teachers who had accompanied me and my mother, but they stayed silent.

'Football,' he waved his hand. 'It's not in our remit.'

And with that he seemed to lose interest and the meeting was over.

'Screw him, screw him and his arrangement,' my mother said once we were outside, her mouth a hard, straight line. 'It's all just a way to get to you, to get you in, it's a trap. We're just going to have to do it without them.'

Not for the first time, I smiled at my mother, the passionate supporter of football. When Samira and I had approached her with our plan to contact other schools, I asked her to come and watch us play one afternoon. She stood watching as we played, as we called out to each other confidently, coordinating where to run and when to pass the ball. She saw the look in our eyes when we scored a goal. Afterwards she came over to Samira and me.

'What we want to do is expand to other schools,' I said. 'To find other girls who want to play.'

She looked at me, and for a moment I was worried that she thought it was too risky. My eyes were still bright from the game, my hair was tousled. She cupped my sweaty face with her hand. 'Well then,' she said. 'That is what we will do.'

Over the following weeks and months, using my mother's connections as a PE teacher, we went into other schools to recruit and expand. Schools that had basketball or volleyball teams would convert to football so they could play against us. We would sneak through the streets to secret matches set up with these other schools, and victory in these football games became a real source of pride for students, who embraced the competitiveness of it. Despite swapping hands for feet, one volleyball team beat us easily. We weren't very good. We didn't train; we just played for the fun of it. There was no real structure or skill to what we did, but that wasn't the point – it was about how it made us feel. We played with whatever we had. Some played barefoot, unflinchingly bouncing across the stone-strewn floor, their feet quickly growing calluses as thick as leather.

It was clear that so many of the girls felt like us. They were desperate for something to claim as their own, for somewhere they could forget about people watching, and instead run, shout, laugh. A momentary respite where the sole objective is to work together to get the ball into the goal. As women, we were all used to our behaviour being monitored and reported, not only by men but by other women. We shared a mutual understanding that being together, cooperating, being on the same team – even if it was just for the duration of a game – felt like a revolutionary act.

Our games were a secret. Most families remained completely unaware of their daughters' involvement. We would manipulate school hours to be able to play, sometimes saying we were unwell and skipping a class to get to a game. There were several schools in close vicinity to each other and we took advantage of their proximity to arrange games on the way to and from school. We would pass each other notes with times and locations.

Gradually, we got more and more organised. We hosted games in our schoolyard and played away at other schools too. The number of adults in the know expanded beyond just my mum. We relied on sympathetic teachers who, in their ones and twos, were supportive. They were protective of us and did everything they could to enable our right to continue playing sport. They pushed back against the attitudes of conservative school principals and made sure we had space to play. Girls who didn't have a team in their school travelled to join in with ours. It reached a point where some schools had to have two teams because so many wanted to participate. There was a real momentum to what we were doing.

It was all operating under the radar until the head of women's football and the head of women's sport for the NOC – essentially tokenistic roles set up for show – got involved. They had received some funding to promote sports in schools and were organising seminars and events in schools across the city. My mum would take me along with her to the sessions. I was desperate to find a way to help girls play in the open rather than underground. I knew that if we were allowed to play legitimately, attitudes towards women would begin to change. I was always the only teenager there, surrounded by teachers, but I was just about old enough to look like my mum's colleague rather than a student. The schoolteachers at these seminars oversaw PE, not because they wanted to or had any professional training in physical education, but because their timetables needed filling. I would go to every workshop I could; especially the ones focusing on basketball and badminton, because I wanted to understand and then coach all sports. During one of these meetings, when I was speaking passionately to the PE teachers about why football was so important, why it was essential that every girl had the opportunity to play if she wanted to, I turned to find my mother watching me, her eyes shining.

In order to attend these conferences and seminars I sometimes had to skip school. The caretakers and cleaners helped me. I would go into class and sit there close to the window. After our attendance was taken at the beginning of the lesson, I would drop my increasingly battered school bag out of the window when the teacher turned her back on us, and one of my accomplices would grab it for me. I would make an excuse, like saying I needed to go to the toilet or felt unwell, and then I'd duck out. My teacher didn't really care whether I came back or not; she would often forget. But I made sure I got top grades, so nobody could discredit football by saying it was bad for a girl's education. Even while I was travelling I would find the time to study, either by not sleeping at all, forcing myself to read deep into the night, or setting an alarm to wake up at 4 a.m. to catch up.

I began to attend conferences in place of my mum, sometimes travelling across the city. She was worried at first, but I explained it would be fine. The first time I did this she quizzed me in detail when I got home. I answered, honestly, that no one seemed to care. I was confident and precocious. They didn't ask me many questions and just assumed I was a teacher, because why else would I be there? I kept a colourful spare scarf tucked in my bag so I could swap it and look less like I was wearing a school uniform.

I felt like some sort of secret agent, on a mission to access information, to understand how the sporting world worked and to make connections. When I met representatives from the NOC, I told them about our underground teams and tournaments. I explained that we played home and away games, that there were rivalries and excitement, and that we had dozens and dozens of girls involved. The next step was to get the Football Federation involved, to have our teams and games officially recognised and legitimised. I didn't know how these things worked. I didn't know the Football Federation and the NOC were separate bodies at that time; I just explained to the NOC representatives that we wanted to have our teams registered so we could select a national team. They listened and explained that the Football Federation was a different body. They told me where it was, but they talked about us taking a small delegation of teachers to discuss it with the president of the NOC. And that's how we found ourselves in the room with Jigdalek and his squeaking chair. We had been building our movement from the bottom up, and now we needed to take action from the top downwards. But our first attempt had been thwarted. We needed a new plan.

At the time, the German Football Association was very supportive of Afghan football. They were very invested in its development, sending coaches and instructors to the country to assist the growth of the sport. I had attended some of the courses run by a German instructor, alongside a few other women and girls. It was incredible to get this perspective on the sport, of what it could be, and to learn more about coaching. I wanted to know how to help a player become better, how to help a group play better as a team, and to understand nutrition, sports science and psychology. The more I learnt, the more I tried to incorporate that knowledge when we played and practised.

After we had completed a course, I was invited to Germany, along with Samira and six others. We were promised official chaperones for the trip for our safety, which helped us to convince our families to let us go. My parents saw it as an opportunity for me to broaden my knowledge and bring back ideas that would further help women and girls in Afghanistan.

It was winter and Germany was cold and dark. We spent all of our time in a sports campus attached to a football club in the middle of nowhere. Nevertheless, I was like a sponge, soaking up everything they taught us. In turn, I told people about the reality of living in Afghanistan as a young woman and of the girls who were playing in the shadows, desperate for support and recognition. Samira and I were as thick as thieves; we had freedom like we'd never had before. We could laugh loudly, shout out our opinions and express ourselves openly. Back home we only behaved this way in secret. This kind of shared, reckless fun – the freedom to be yourself – was alien to how we lived back in Afghanistan, and our newfound freedom bonded us even more.

We were astonished to find that when we went out, no one paid attention to us at all. Nobody cared how we dressed. Samira even joked that she was a little bit disappointed, but really, we all felt refreshed by this newfound freedom, this ability to walk around without the pervasive watchful gaze and judgement of others. The women who came to our training sessions and worked with us were so powerful and full of life. They didn't seem to be preoccupied with monitoring themselves; they were relaxed and open. We weren't used to seeing women who carried themselves in such a way, who were so respected and influential.

'What do you think it's like to live here?' I asked Samira one day, as we took a bus through the streets, watching people walking hand in hand and laughing. The women were so loud and confident, and they didn't care who was watching them.

'It's different,' said Samira. 'Everyone behaves differently here. Society is just different and that's normal to them.' She shrugged. 'But it always rains and the food is better back home.'

We noticed that Germany was less sociable in some ways too: strangers didn't interact with each other in the street like they did in Afghanistan. Of course we enjoyed our new freedoms, but being removed from the culture of our country enabled us to see some of the things we loved about it, and not just the things we didn't.

When I returned home, I eagerly told my mother what I had learnt, using objects on the dinner table to illustrate my points. 'I don't know what any of this means,' she laughed. 'But it's very impressive.'

The next day I went into school and was walking down the corridor when I heard a voice shout: 'Whore!' I looked up and saw two male members of staff looking at me with contempt. That is how I realised they knew about my trip to Germany. Attitudes on the ground were still very conservative, despite the new Western-backed government pushing for change from the top. To them, to be involved in sport as a woman meant that I must be Western and not an honourable woman. I was corrupting myself by indulging in sport. If I was willing to do that then what else was I doing? I must be promiscuous; I must surely have no honour.

That afternoon in class, after we had practised in the yard, I became aware of the school director, a thin angular woman in her fifties, leaning down over me and sniffing. As always I had sprayed myself with perfume to hide the stench of sweat that I was so paranoid about. Now she reached into my bag and took out the bottle of perfume. Then, she slapped me hard in the face. I was so shocked I didn't do anything. She grabbed hold of my hair and dragged me to my feet in front of my astonished classmates. 'You are a whore,' she said, her voice rising until she was shouting in my face. 'You dishonour your mother and your father. You dishonour your classmates and the entire school.' She took me to sit in the school office and left me there for the entire day, so that I missed the whole class.

Later that week, I was helping the school's window cleaner, as I sometimes did. He only had a small piece of torn cloth and would have to stretch his hunched body to reach the top of the glass. He was old and his hands never seemed to stop shaking. So, when no one was looking, I would go and help him. Sometimes I took over entirely so he could give his stretched and aching muscles some respite. Helping him reminded me of when I used to work with my grandfather. This time, as I was reaching up to one of the windows, I heard a shout from behind me. A teacher was racing in my direction, calling my name and screaming at me. She grabbed my hair in one hand and my arm in the other and dragged me towards my classmates. My back arched as my head was yanked backwards by the force of her grip on my hair. She slapped me in the face for helping the cleaner and told me that it wasn't my job. It was just an excuse; I was being targeted. I was facing more and more aggression in school every day.

I didn't know it at the time, but I found out later that they also gave my mum a hard time. She didn't fight back; she would just stay silent and cry. I could see the pain it caused her. She looked weary and defeated. In almost every staff meeting my upbringing would be questioned and teachers would imply that I was a prostitute. No one challenged the accusations and no one asked for any evidence. There obviously wouldn't have been any, but it was the school director leading the charge and so no one dared question it. My mum shielded me from this, but they sought to shame her, to break her. They thought breaking her would bring me in line. If they broke her, surely she would retaliate and clamp down on my behaviour. Instead, she continued to quietly support me in creating a network of women who were teaching sport to girls.

Schools knew they had to be seen to be offering opportunities to girls, but they didn't take those initiatives seriously. Gradually, a group of like-minded women came together and discussed what could be done to force the hands of the men in power. One day, one of them suggested that we just turn up at the Football Federation, unannounced: 'What are they going to do, have us physically removed?'

So my mother and I, along with two other female teachers, went to the Football Federation building and announced to the puzzled receptionist that we were here for a meeting with the president. From our research, we knew that Abdul Alim Gen. Maj. Kohistani was an extremist and very religious. He was a military man, with good connections throughout the government, and we were nervous as we waited to be called in. As we walked through the building to his office, we didn't see a single woman. The whole place smelt of cigarette smoke and unwashed bodies. It felt oppressive. By this point a couple of years had passed since the Taliban lost power, but that meant nothing to men like Kohistani. We knew the truth. They were present everywhere in buildings like this.

Kohistani was sitting at his desk when we entered. He did not stand up to greet us. He was heavyset, with dark features and the shadow of a beard around his face. He barely looked at us. He just gestured for us to sit down. I noticed a large, expensive-looking ring on his finger as he did so.

'OK, what do you want?' he said, finally.

I began the same speech I had given the president of the NOC: that we had established several school teams and we wanted recognition, we wanted support to encourage more girls into football, and we wanted a national women's team. I did not mention the words 'women's rights' or 'human rights' – I knew the moment we mentioned these things it would be game over. Any suggestion of this being about women's empowerment would lead to it being stamped down on hard. We played innocent: we wanted to help more girls play sport so that the international community would look kindly upon our country.

'You know, we already have the men's team, who are a huge embarrassment. Do you think we are ready to have a women's team too?' he said. The recent failure of the men's national team was proving a hurdle to our cause. The team had travelled to play against Iran and lost badly, and it was all over the news that they had been bullied and humiliated in Iran. They were a laughing stock. 'We are still suffering from the men bringing embarrassment to our country. Now we have to deal with you wanting to bring more. If you win – embarrassment. If you lose – embarrassment. You see my predicament.'

He looked at us, unsmiling, with his hands outstretched. 'We have a reputation and a good name. I think it is better for everyone if the women of our country concentrate on education, not wasting time on sport.'

With that he looked away and the meeting was over.

I wasn't going to give up. I went back to school frustrated but undeterred. I was convinced that there had to be a way back in. Over the next few months, we got in touch with more schools across the region. We kept recruiting more girls, determined to do whatever we could to make it impossible for the football authorities to ignore us. When our parents thought we were doing homework, Samira and I would spend hours discussing what we could do to find more and more girls. We would meet with them on the way to or from school, telling them how to talk to their teachers and their parents, what to say, what had worked with others. It was a kind of coaching – not about how to play football, but about how to earn the right to play it.

When a new president of the Football Federation was instated – a man by the name of Keramuddin Karim – we turned up for another meeting. The same building, the same smell of old sweat and cigarettes. But, this time, we decided on a different strategy: it was no good trying to get their attention by talking about the welfare of women and girls – they simply didn't care. We had to appeal to their greed.

Keramuddin Karim was another hulking man, a warlord whose hairline looked like it was trying to leave via the back of his head, which was balanced on top of roll after roll of chin. He was notorious for having had numerous affairs. He had worked in the defence ministry beforehand, where he had gained a reputation for being a harasser and an abuser of women.

In the meeting, I spoke at length about travelling to Germany, about how I had seen first-hand the money and potential profits that could be made in women's football. How it would attract Western investment, which could be reinvested in the men's team or how the federation saw fit; how we needed very little from them, other than the explicit permission to set up the national team and find players for it; how, in exchange, they would get good publicity and money. At the end of my speech, he was watching me with a strange look of amusement and curiosity.

'Of course, there is nothing I can do to support you,' he said. 'But I won't stop you.'

That was all we needed.

6

To be part of a team is to be reminded that you matter. To be relied upon and to rely on others. To feel that you exist. When your team scores and you run to greet each other, shouting in joy, you are calling out to each other, 'I am here! I am *here*!' Open your eyes.

The striker raced towards the goal, but the player between the temporary goalposts was calm, steady. She was tall, with naturally white-blonde hair. She waited and waited, and then, at just the right moment, dived to the ground and blocked the incoming ball. You could tell immediately that she had played before. She had been coached by a real coach.

'Who are you and where did you learn how to do that?' I shouted, running over to her.

'Hi, I'm Dahmina. In Italy,' she said, grinning. Something about the way she stood there struck me. She didn't look afraid. She looked like she belonged.

'Well, I think we've found our goalkeeper,' said Samira, writing on her clipboard. I came to learn that Dahmina and her family had fled Afghanistan when the Taliban came into power, just as my family and I had, but instead of Pakistan they had gone to Italy. Even there it had been tricky for Dahmina to play football, as her family were very religious and strict, but she lived for it. Any time she could, she would sneak out to play. Returning to Afghanistan when she was sixteen, she experienced the same culture shock as I had, but she found solace and comfort in football.

After our meeting with the president of the Football Federation, we realised that without support there was no way we could travel around the country sourcing players. Instead, we needed an efficient way of getting the players to come to us. We decided that the best way to find players for the team was to host a big tournament. We had already received the most important concession, which was that the authorities wouldn't actually stop us. So, the secret network we had been building up sprang into action: we made posters that were put up in the local schools, we contacted schools across the country and we tried to spread the word as far as possible, despite a lack of resources and support from senior staff in these institutions. We plastered the name of the Football Federation over every poster and flyer to legitimise our cause and we invited members of the federation along.

On the morning of the tournament, we arrived at the school grounds an hour earlier than was advertised, to set up. There were already about a hundred girls waiting. I gripped Samira's hand tightly with excitement. We took down their names and addresses and quickly realised that everyone was from Kabul. This mean that the tournament wouldn't be representative of the whole country, but it was a start.

The few members of the Football Federation who turned up were clearly puzzled by what was happening, but we told them they could put their name to the tournament and claim the work as their own. They could soak up the plaudits for championing women's football and have their photos taken, all without lifting a finger. We knew that they would find it impossible to resist being hailed as trailblazers and applauded for our successes. We also knew that they would then find it harder to back away from or withdraw support for the team down the line.

We divided the players into eight teams and they began to play. There was a massive range of ability. Some had barely ever touched a ball before, but others were skilful, and then there were the odd few who had clearly received some coaching. Every single one of them was taking a risk by being there, and they all burnt with passion in exercising their right to play football. As the day went on, Samira and I and some of the sports teachers walked around, watching the games and pulling together a list of potential players. Slowly we began to piece together enough names for a team and then a squad of twenty-two players.

At the end of the day, we got everyone together and read out a list of the players who we wanted to attend the first training session the following week. It was a success: we finally had a team. But we had no coach and nowhere to play. So back to the federation we went.

This time Karim was clearly annoyed that we were beginning to build momentum.

'It is impossible,' he said. 'There is nowhere that would be . . . suitable for women to be seen playing a game like this.'

'What about the Women's Garden?' said one of the teachers. The Kabul Women's Garden was a gated park where only women and male children under nine were permitted entry. There were flower gardens and trees and paths between them, as well as shops and gyms and classrooms, all run by women.

'But there isn't a football pitch there,' I pointed out. 'Only a tennis court.'

'Very well,' said Karim, shuffling papers to signify the meeting was over. 'But you cannot take the net down.'

In the time following the tournament I also had regular meetings with a group of female sports teachers to discuss a strategy, and in the evenings I would meet with Samira to develop a plan for building the team from the top down. In most countries, there is a healthy grassroots league system representing teams across the nation: players compete locally and the best teams play each other, as do school teams. Some countries even have semi-professional and professional teams to draw their players from. But we didn't have any of that infrastructure in place. We needed to work backwards and use the profile of a recognised national team to empower women at the grassroots level. Our plan was to start with the senior side and then expand the national team set-up to include youth teams, holding regular festivals and tournaments to recruit for different age groups.

A few days after our meeting with Karim, Samira and I arrived at the small tennis court in the corner of the garden. 'It's a start,' she said.

And so, we began to train. At first the women were shy around each other, hesitant. They were clearly unsure if they could trust us, or each other. They were used to their behaviour being monitored and feared the risk of it being reported back to their families. But gradually, as the sessions continued, they began to relax and take up space. Their voices grew louder and they began to talk about things other than football.

One day, a girl named Damsa, a powerful and talented left back, turned up to one of the training sessions visibly upset. When pressed she told us that she had been beaten by her brother because she had wanted to rush off to football before she'd finished washing the dishes. She had twisted free of him and got to training, but she didn't know what she would return to. The other girls nodded along, tutting in sympathy. 'Fucker,' said Samira sharply, and the girls looked at her. 'Fucker', said Damsa, and the women laughed.

Another time, one of the girls admitted that she had no idea what her extended family would do if they found out she was playing football. If they decided that her dishonour reflected on them, it would be their responsibility to punish her. Yet again,

I was reminded how lucky I was to have the family I did. My father would check in on Samira and me when we were supposed to be doing our homework but were actually planning training sessions. He would nod and smile with a twinkle in his eye when we told him we were studying physics. The thought that these girls went home to fathers and brothers who would beat them, to mothers and sisters who would nod along, broke my heart.

Some of the girls spoke of how their families were starting to talk about marital arrangements. We all feared being pushed into marriage, potentially at an early age. We would share our dreams, fears and experiences, and suggest solutions to our teammates; we would strategise on delaying tactics. I shared the ways I would make it difficult when my mother and grandmother brought men home to meet me: I would be late, act rudely and do my utmost to put the man off. Some girls spoke to their families, arguing that they should be educated and not married young in order to protect them from a life of poverty should something happen to their husbands, brothers or fathers. They played up fears of poverty and prostitution to highlight the positives of education. What worked for one could work for another, so we all shared strategies for how to approach situations.

Samira and I encouraged the girls to talk to their parents in a language they would understand, highlighting how many men had died or been killed through living in a war-torn country and how important it therefore was for women to be educated and work. One idea we formulated collectively was that we would go as a team to speak to a family to convince them to allow their daughters to play if they were concerned. We would dress well, be polite and appeal on their behalf, attempting to demonstrate that we were good women for their daughters to be around.

We never knew what would be waiting for us back home when we weren't together, making the time we spent on the pitch all the more special and joyful, because it was a refuge for us all. Slowly, the training pitch revealed itself as a new place: a home of trust and growing sisterhood, a place where the players could be themselves, away from oppressive societal expectations. We told jokes, we celebrated. We all took off our headscarves and felt the air moving through our hair. We coached each other on and off the pitch, and Samira was the heart of all of it: her football knowledge guided us on the pitch and her quiet brilliance off the field was infectious.

Gradually we gained a firmer sense of our starting eleven too. At the end of one session, I told Dahmina that she was our first choice for goalkeeper, and watched as tears silently rolled down her cheeks. We had come to know her as a joker: if there was ever laughter, Dahmina would be at the centre of it. It was rare to see displays of emotion from her, but she was clearly overcome by the news. Outside of the Women's Garden, our faces were shrouded by burqas and scarves, but in this women-only space we could drop our masks and so I could see the tears flowing down Dahmina's face. They were tears of joy but also of pain. She admitted that she still hadn't told her family.

That evening, I went to my mother and told her we needed to help some of the players tell their families. Part of me was worried that she would find this confrontation too dangerous. She had been so supportive, but I knew that surely I would reach a point where her support would falter. My mother rubbed her eyes, her weariness and wariness evident. I knew that many of the girls we had selected were playing football completely in secret. There was no way we could keep that going.

'Well then,' my mother said. 'Let's go and do that.'

Dahmina's family sat in silence, looking back at us.

'I have only one daughter,' my mother said. 'If I felt this was something dangerous, I wouldn't let my daughter play, but it helps her in so many ways, academically and socially.'

They looked, confusedly, at the group of women sitting in their front room: myself, my mum and Dahmina. When we revealed Dahmina's talent their shock was palpable, and we of course masked much of the deception that had led us to this point. We appealed for her to be able to take part with their agreement, if not their full approval. We explained that it was a women-led initiative, that it was a movement that brought women together and encouraged support and unity. And we made it clear that it was not an anti-man initiative but was instead about women coming together to support inclusion and create more opportunities for women. It was difficult to read the faces of her father and brother. They listened quietly, but there was an unpleasantness to the air and to their expressions. Then Dahmina's father stood up.

'You are prostitutes!' he yelled. 'You have shamed your own families and now you have come here to recruit my daughter into prostitution. Get out before I show you what the men of your family should have done a long time ago!'

We sat for a moment in shock.

'Get out, I said!'

He gestured wildly with his hands and Dahmina's brothers stood up to flank their father. We backed out of the house with our hands held up in surrender, and all the while they were cursing us. I could see Dahmina's petrified eyes in the background. I knew that other girls had been beaten badly when their families had found out. As we walked away from their house, my mother held my hand tightly. She was shaking, but I couldn't tell if it was from anger or fear. We didn't speak, and neither of us told my father what had happened when we returned home.

At the next training session, as we had expected, Dahmina wasn't present. One of the other girls went to her school and found out that she had attended her lessons, but was being shepherded to and from school by her brothers. It was too dangerous to try and contact her directly and we knew that doing so could even make things worse for her. So we decided to play the long game. We had spoken to three other families about their daughters' involvement in the team. Two of them remained polite but forbade their daughters from continuing to play, and one family had been comforted by my mother's arguments.

The following few weeks were especially intense, as we were training once a week in addition to the games we were playing at school and I was studying for my final exams. I barely had time to stop and eat. I was also trying to read everything I could about sports coaching. The more I played and coached our team, the more I saw the power of football to rebuild the trust among people that had been decimated by the Taliban. I threw myself into training even more enthusiastically, demanding more and more from the players. For this to work, we had to grow and play to the best of our abilities. That would be the only route into other adventures.

One week, I waited for Samira to come and help me during a training session, but she never arrived. I felt annoyed. 'Has anyone heard from Samira?' I asked the other girls. They shook their heads.

A couple of days later at school I found her. She tried to avoid me by turning and walking away.

'Hey, where were you?' I said angrily. 'We can't stop pushing now, we're so close.'

'Please,' she said, her voice catching. 'Please don't.' The life had disappeared from her eyes. 'My father found out,' she said.

I instinctively reached out to touch her arm gently, to comfort her, but she recoiled and winced.

'But we can't have a team without our playmaker,' I said, trying to smile at her. 'Who's going to find those passes?'

She just shook her head and tried to leave.

'You and Dahmina are our best players,' I said.

She stopped, turned and gave me a look that sent a chill down my spine.

'Khalida,' she said, in a different voice. Her tone was different. Low and defeated. 'You haven't heard, have you?'

Dahmina had defied her parents when she came to the tournament to try out for the national team. They had already banned her from playing football at school after they found out she was staying behind to practise. She was so desperate to play she would sneak out to join the national team sessions, pretending to be studying late at school or at a friend's house. When her parents found out that she had ignored their instruction for her to stop, they took away every freedom she had, caging her within their home and relentlessly beating her, trying to break her spirit. By stopping her from leaving the house and taking away football, they took away her joy, her love and her motivation. Football was the only thing that had kept her believing that there was more for her than marriage, children and a life of obedience and servitude.

We weren't there to see what happened, but we all heard about it. It was a useful story – a warning to girls like me who dared to think bigger than what society in Afghanistan told us was our lot. So, adults didn't mind the story spreading. Since her parents stole football from her, Dahmina stole some fuel from them, dowsing herself in it before striking a match and setting herself alight. It was the last thing she could control. If she couldn't control how she lived, she could control how she died.

One evening, a few weeks after Dahmina's funeral, which we could not attend, I received a call on my first mobile phone, from a boy I had met playing badminton. Without thinking, I answered it in front of my parents. As soon as I got off the phone I noticed my dad was very uncomfortable. I tried to explain that the boy had just called me up to ask something completely innocent, but my dad just kept shaking his head.

'Too many, Khalida. You are going through too many red lights.' I asked him what he meant. 'Enough is enough, it's time to stop this and focus on your studies.' Again I asked him what he meant. 'Playing at school, OK fine. But going away, to conferences, to meetings, to tournaments, to other countries, and stirring up these other girls with promises of a team. It is getting too much.' He said that too many people knew I was involved in sport. I was putting myself at greater and greater risk and he wanted me to step aside to focus on getting into university. He thought that sport would get me nowhere in our community, in our world; it offered few opportunities, and it wasn't safe. Home had always been a sanctuary for me, but there was danger outside and it felt ever present.

Traditionally, the women in my family would already be married or about to be wed by my age. Instead, I was playing football, travelling alone and engaging in debates. By simply being me, I was promoting the idea that there is more for women in the world. I was the opposite of traditional expectations, including my own family's, on both my mother's side and my father's side. I tried to appeal to my mother, to reason with her, to understand what was happening. 'Family is family,' is all she would say. I got the sense that rumours had been spreading and that there was pressure on my parents from members of our extended family to bring me in line.

The next day, I was about to leave for training as usual when my father called me to him. He said I wasn't allowed to go. I argued back: 'Why?' I protested. And then he said something he had never said before.

'I am the father of this house. My money allows your freedoms and I am the one in charge. I have to think of the whole family.'

I was taken aback, but I noticed for the first time the frustration and despair in the lines on his weary face. I wondered what names he had heard me being called. I knew he had defended me, again and again, but I needed him to support me now more than ever.

'You risked everything for me to have an education and have freedoms and now you're preventing me from doing the very things that you have told me to do?' I said. 'You are no better than the Taliban. You're preventing me from doing what I want to do just because you are my dad, because you're scared that something could happen to me or that I could lose my life, but *nowhere* in Afghanistan is safe. Everything I do is dangerous. Football can get me shot, harassed, abused or killed, but so can going to school or walking in the street. There is always risk. This country is dangerous. No matter how you live, even if you're married and at home, violence can still find you. We don't just give up and do nothing just because it's dangerous, or we would never do anything at all.'

It didn't matter what I said, he wouldn't relent. He told me to go to my room and stay there until he sent for me.

I felt like the bars were coming up over the windows and the door was being locked. My dad was threatening to take away the thing that mattered most to me. I didn't want to argue any more. I didn't want to have daily conflicts with my dad, the same ones my teammates were having with their families. I saw the toll that it was taking on everyone. I felt as though my purpose was being ripped from me. Life didn't feel worth living any more. My soul was being taken away, so why should my body still live, wandering around devoid of purpose and joy?

I quietly crept along the hall to the cabinet where we kept different medicines, and I took whatever I could take. My mother found me not long after, unconscious.

I was taken to a hospital. My stomach was pumped. My face was swollen. For weeks I slept and whenever I woke, my mother was sitting by my bed, watching me.

7

Islamabad, 2007

There is a moment when you feel you are becoming a team. There is a kind of magic to this feeling. Like singing, or dancing, or falling in love. It happens as you make yourself vulnerable through trust, through trying your hardest and through relying, absolutely, on others. Open your eyes.

'Hey! Hey, pass!'

Maryam was running, waving her arms for the pass, but it never came. So, giving up, she stood with her arms crossed as the ball was smuggled out of play.

'What the hell is the matter with her?' she said, shaking her head as I caught up to her.

'Coach!' I shouted, walking to the sideline where a figure was sitting, wearing dark glasses under a baseball cap. 'Coach?' I said again as I got closer.

He jerked upright and I realised he had been asleep.

Since returning from the hospital, I had only attended a couple of training sessions, and my father hadn't raised the issue of me being involved with football. We hadn't explicitly discussed it, but he had clearly realised there was no way I was going to be stopped from chasing this goal. I suspected my mother had been lobbying on my behalf.

It was a good thing too, as I returned to the news that the team had been invited to play our first ever international game, in Pakistan, as a guest team in a new, small tournament. It was our biggest victory yet. Federations around the world were starting to get more money for women's football from FIFA and so the sport was growing in a number of countries. Pakistan was further along in their journey than we were; they already had a national league. FIFA had arranged for us to play our first game against the Pakistan national team in Islamabad. Most importantly, it meant that – even if only to save face – the Football Federation would have to be seen to be doing some of the basics. Including, appointing a coach for the first time.

It had only taken fifteen minutes of our first training session for me to realise what was going on. Our new coach had played football in the Afghan league. He was good-looking and physically fit and he knew it. Rather than seeming to care at all about training us, he treated that first session as a social occasion, flirting with the players, eyeing their bodies as they stretched.

'Coach,' I said at one point. 'How do you want us to play?'

He looked puzzled for a moment, as if he'd entirely forgotten why he was there.

'Oh, I'm sure you'll play beautifully,' he said, not even bothering to conceal his gaze as he watched one of the player's legs. 'Just beautifully.'

The past few months had been lonely without Samira and Dahmina. They had always been the closest to my sense of humour and I missed them. I had hoped that Samira would find a way to return to playing football. But she never did. Every time I saw her, it was in the distance, with one of her male relatives in close attendance. I realised they didn't have to physically do anything to make you disappear.

But one positive thing was that I had become closer to Maryam. As I spent more time with Maryam and our friendship grew, I began to rely on her. She was tiny, strong and fast, and had learnt to play with boys in the grounds of the orphanage she grew up in. Her family lived in the mountains but had been unable to afford to feed her, so she lived in the orphanage. Walking into the foothills of the mountains to visit her parents had helped her to build strong muscles. She was a pacey, raw winger with a dry sense of humour, and she would rage constantly at the men who controlled football in our country. She would do an impression of our new playboy coach that made us both howl with laughter.

In the upcoming tournament in Pakistan, we would be playing eight games against teams from the newly formed Pakistan women's league. We trained hard, to try and be ready for our first ever international game. But all the while, I couldn't get rid of the feeling that our coach was making selections based more on the basis of who he had taken a shine to and who laughed at his jokes rather than what was best for the team. The only good thing was that he spent the bare minimum of time with the team.

Getting permission from our families to travel was extremely complicated. Some of the players didn't tell their families until they were already travelling, and others didn't tell their parents at all. There were complex plans, with sympathetic relatives, usually women – aunts, sisters and mothers – coordinating cover for the absent players. We travelled out a week early, so we would have time to practise and prepare.

One of the first things we did was visit the Jinnah Sports Stadium in Islamabad, where we would be playing. The players whistled at how big the pitch was, gazing around at the almost fifty thousand brightly coloured seats that surrounded us. Our goalkeeper went and stood in one of the goals and tried in vain to jump and touch the crossbar.

'It's a long way from the tennis court, hey?' I called out, and she made a face.

We tottered across the running track that circled the pitch, slipping as if on ice. We had never worn boots with studs before. Most of us usually wore boots that didn't fit, as the Football Federation had sourced them without finding out what size feet any of us had. Mine pinched my little toe. Here, we were given our first proper kit.

At our first training session in Pakistan, our coach stayed for about half an hour, just long enough to make a joke about one of the players being a natural up front, while staring at her chest. Several of the players laughed nervously. She crossed her arms, looking mortified. Just before he left, to go shopping for his wife and children, he had an intense conversation with one of the female teachers who had accompanied us. Afterwards, she came over to me and said, 'These shirts are completely see-through.' I realised she was right. The material was so thin and of such poor quality that there was no way we would be able to wear them without another layer underneath.

With our coach not around – and pretty much useless when he occasionally was – we coached ourselves. We had no idea what would happen in the game, so we spent the week getting used to playing on a full-size pitch. We ran and ran, staying in our formation, with the right distances between us. Before long, the day of the match was upon us.

In truth, we were terrified: scared by the huge expanse of grass, by the huge gaping mouths of the goals, ready to swallow us up. We walked out trembling, already sweating from the double layers we were wearing. There was no crowd. Women's football was a sport hardly anyone knew even existed, let alone supported, so only the officials and event organisers were present. Despite being with my teammates, in that moment I felt so unbearably lonely. Our kits may have been lightweight, but the badge we cherished felt heavy. What were we doing? What were we thinking? How on earth could we play for a full 90 minutes on a pitch like this? Against a Pakistan club team, who were so much more experienced than us? All the joy I felt when I played football was being sapped away by the pressure of needing to prove ourselves. We were far from home, defying everything our society expected of women, yet it felt like we had been set up to fail – and we would fail big time. The emotions that raced through us were many, ranging from embarrassment and fear to frustration and anger.

But when the first notes of the Afghanistan national anthem began to play through crackling speakers, the mood in our ranks shifted from despair to pride. It rushed up through my body, tingling from my toes up to the top of my head and bursting out of me. I blinked, trying to force back the tears that were building in the corners of my eyes, but instead sending them cascading down my cheeks. The national anthem grounded me. The flag of my country flew high and my heart soared with it. Standing in the national stadium of a country where I had spent my most formative years, a place I had once adopted and then had to leave, I felt more connected to my homeland than ever before. I took all of the frustration and the anger at every obstacle put in our way, the rage at everyone who was denying women and girls the opportunity to play, and used it for the battle before us.

When the whistle blew, everything else vanished. My ears switched off to any sound beyond the pitch. I felt like I was in a bubble that only the whistle at the end of the match could burst. We weren't good – we lacked technique and skills and our fitness levels were non-existent – but we had heart. We ran and ran in boots that didn't fit and shirts that tore and had to be changed on the touchline. And we laughed. We ran and laughed and ran, until we could barely take a breath.

'Well, that wasn't fun,' said Maryam.

The team was sitting in my room, players wincing, slumped around like soldiers after a military defeat. It had been painful: 4–0 in the end. We hadn't known how to cope with a team who were far better trained than us. We didn't know where to stand or run. We found ourselves chasing the ball around the pitch, as they calmly passed through us. As a defender it was my job to stop the other team scoring, but they were too quick. As one of us chased the ball, it left a gap that one of the others had to fill. I realised how different the game was on the field and on a whiteboard. As goal after goal went in, I could see players forcing back tears of frustration and humiliation. The only positive was that not one of us gave up. We kept running, we kept trying. I saw the strength in all of us. But now, I was filled with anger at how this strength wasn't being utilised.

I left the room and marched along the corridor to our coach's room. I could hear the low murmuring of voices and laughter, then silence as I knocked on the door. After a long pause, the door opened and the coach stood peering out, his face flushed. 'Ah yes, Khalida, of course,' he said. 'How can I help?' His eyes were twinkling and mischievous.

'You can coach us,' I said. 'We didn't know where to stand or where to run. We need you to tell us what to do, to give us a strategy, a formation, anything.'

He glanced up and down the corridor at my raised voice. His face hardened and he stepped out towards me, closing the door a little behind him.

'It doesn't matter,' he said.

'What?' I said, shocked.

'It doesn't matter where you stand or how you run, what formation you use, or tactics, or anything. It doesn't matter whether you win or lose. Whatever happens, you will be celebrated in the West and you will bring shame on yourselves at home. And I will be stuck here until the federation decides to stop punishing me and give me a real job.' He finished almost snarling. Then, in an instant, he was smiling again. 'Now, my advice to all of you would be to go to sleep,' he said, waving me away with his hand. 'Recovery is very important.'

With that he shut the door in my face. I heard the sound of someone shifting on a bed and low laughter.

I returned to the hotel room. That night I sat with the rest of the team and we came up with a game plan. Our lack of footballing knowledge was felt acutely in the room. We had no strategy, we had no real understanding of the tactical side of the game. All we could come up with was that we had to fight to the end and not give up. No matter how tough it got, no matter what the scoreline, we would support and fight for each other. We discussed our overall purpose as a group. We concluded that the recent defeat was only one game; it was far from the be-all and end-all. We felt incredibly vulnerable. We were ready to be humbled further, but we were also ready to hide any weakness. We would not cry; we would not display any signs that we felt embarrassed. We would just do our best and keep fighting, for each other.

The next day, in the first game of that tournament, against one of the club teams who were less developed than the country's marginally more advanced national team, we showed signs of improvement. Everyone got one pass, and that was a good start – for us. Our strategy was far from complex: make sure the ball goes the right way and protect the goal.

It sounds silly, amateur, like we were in a playground working out the rules of the game for the first time, but in a way we were. Some of us had done basic courses and had some understanding, but we had never needed to implement tactics against a proper opponent. We had given up on our coach entirely; it was common knowledge that he was regularly in his hotel room with one of the female teachers who had accompanied us. We told him to go and enjoy himself and to leave us to do our thing. We had to learn football while we played football: don't resort to pulling at players, avoid yellow cards and being sent off. We couldn't afford to be a player down; we needed everybody. Those of us who had even a little training were trying to take the lead and sound authoritative, but we didn't really know what we were doing.

This time, as the national anthem played, I sensed a quiet determination. The whistle blew.

'Shit,' said Maryam. 'But less shit.'

She was right. We had lost, but we at least deserved to be on the same pitch as the other team. We dragged our aching limbs to bed, determined to do better the next game. We were all so close and we wanted it so badly. We were driven by solidarity with each other, solidarity with the women of Afghanistan who could benefit from any level of success, and by a love of the game and the freedom it brought us.

Before our third game, I sensed a strange sense of calm, as we got used to being on the pitch. As I looked around at the players before the whistle blew, I sensed them leaning forward, eager for the game to begin.

We knew we had to start winning. The pressure, and the physical and emotional demands of the tournament, were so huge that a number of us vomited before the game. If we lost and returned to Afghanistan embarrassed and in disgrace, we knew we would never play again. We were united by that pressure, and we were a different team because of it. We had to prove to ourselves, our families and our country that the sacrifices we had made mattered. In this game, we were different people when we entered the stadium. We were so much better, we were in sync. We knew we needed to protect our goal, we knew we couldn't concede and we defended as a team. We were really motivating and pushing each other; everyone was a captain. The game was physically tough and we suffered many injuries, but we just played on.

My thigh was black by the end because I had ruptured something under the skin. I was told by a doctor not to play, but I said, 'No, that's not possible, I have to.'

That was our mindset: 'If you lose a leg, you play with one.'

'That,' said Maryam, 'was possibly the best thing ever.'

We had won. By one goal, which Maryam had scored. Maryam, our tricky number nine who we called our Ronaldo. As it hit the net, I found myself running, almost outside of my body, to join the others, who were running too, screaming. It provoked feelings I didn't know existed. Euphoria. Love. A love for football, for my sisters, for life. I could see that the others felt it too as we engulfed each other in a huddle of arms, legs, melting shirts and sweaty bodies, allowing ourselves to lose control after the ball had hit the back of the net.

We won the next game too. We made it to the quarter-finals. Our shirts were falling apart, and we had to keep changing them. Any minor contact or grab from a fellow teammate and the cheap red fabric would tear. The numbers on them had all but vanished as whatever they had used to print them on the shirts dissolved in sweat. We ran until we couldn't run any more, throwing our bodies in the way of shots.

We began to trust each other. We didn't all chase the ball, but rather stayed in our area of the pitch. We even began to find a way to play the ball through our opponents. I could see the confidence begin to fill the team, like a kite beginning to rise in the wind. We managed to win the quarter-final, and at the final whistle we exploded in joy, embracing each other. I sank to my knees and shouted with a mixture of joy and relief, releasing so many years of frustration.

As we left the pitch, I spotted a camera crew and asked who they were. They told me they were a local broadcaster. One of them smiled and said, 'Everyone will be celebrating that you're in the semi-final, right? What an amazing story.' He then explained to me that the game would be available to stream in Afghanistan.

That night, as we celebrated in one of the rooms, I broke the news to the team. The mood changed instantly. Part of me hadn't wanted to tell them. I didn't want to dampen our success by the sudden reality of how we might be perceived back home. After all, what did we have to be ashamed of? Our reactions, our joy and our unity were all natural and there for everyone to see. Anyone who watched would be able to see our pride and passion, and anyone who had opposed, abused and ostracised us would see us triumphant, with the badges on our chests. We had been told for so long that we didn't belong, but there we were. We were proving that the seemingly impossible was possible, and that was such a powerful message. We were making history, a beautiful piece of it that would be nestled within the country's trajectory of despair, war and pain. But players began to worry about being seen, and the risk it would involve for them and their families.

I stood up and looked everyone in the room dead in the eye. 'If playing in the game tomorrow is too much of a risk for any of you, then say so now and we will all understand. None of us expected to win a single game. We didn't expect anyone to care.'

I waited but no one spoke up. Instead, I saw only looks of resolution on their faces.

Back home in Afghanistan there was huge interest in the semi-final. The game was being broadcast again, this time by some of the country's own national media that had travelled to Islamabad after the news of our exploits and success spread. At one point, our coach brought in a phone and put it on loudspeaker. It was the president of Afghanistan, Hamid Karzai.

'We are all proud of you,' he said. 'The whole country. You are the brave Lionesses of Afghanistan. Good luck for your next game.'

As I looked around at the team, I could see a mixture of excitement but also fear.

'Well, we'd better not screw this up,' whispered Maryam.

We were all genuinely scared of how big things were getting, of the exposure and even of how seriously we were being taken. The risk grew with every escalation in interest too. We didn't quite understand what was going on, why it was happening or why we were provoking so much interest when for years we had been made to feel like we didn't belong and people had actively gone out of their way – even as far as assaulting us – to prevent us from playing. We had momentum, but no control over it.

By this point, all our families were watching. It was incredibly weird, but it also showed how powerful us playing could be.

We had no idea what the reactions of our families would be, but they had tuned in to watch. People we knew who didn't know we played football saw our faces on TV screens and in newspapers.

When we won the semi-final and went through to the final, the buzz stepped up another gear. We didn't even know the gears went that high. More media arrived and our profiles were skyrocketing.

Ahead of the final, we plotted our strategy. With so many eyes on us we had to be protective and shield each other from embarrassment or pain. We agreed beforehand that if a player went down with an injury, we would come together in a huddle to shield their anguish and tears from the cameras. We would share our injuries in private, but we would not have images of perceived weakness or impropriety going out to the world. We didn't want to give our detractors the fuel they needed to argue that sport was unsuitable for women.

We were all so nervous. Some of the girls had religious trinkets hidden in their bras and would pray before kick-off. I didn't have time for that, but I was somewhat jealous that they believed a higher power would protect us. We weren't scared of the football any more, or the pitch, or the 90 minutes, but we feared the pressure we were under, to keep proving ourselves and our worth. We knew that the overwhelming majority of those watching wanted us to fail. We knew that our own Football Federation wanted us to fail, because it would give them an excuse to rip up and dispose of the seedling of women's football that we had planted in the hard, stony and unwelcoming ground. They wanted us to embarrass ourselves and embarrass them so they would feel vindicated in their prejudicial views that we were not good enough. That was what fuelled us to fight on through any pain, to prove them wrong. We could have had broken bones or kept running until we passed out – we would have played on regardless.

The president of the Football Federation flew in for the final. People from the Afghanistan Embassy in Islamabad came to watch too, along with a number of Afghans who lived in the capital. The crowd swelled far beyond the few that had watched the preceding games, much larger than any crowd we had ever played in front of before. It felt unreal, as if we were caught in some sort of fable. We had to win.

I could feel my chest rising and falling; the noise of the bustling crowd was replaced by the sound of my ragged breathing. The nerves were crippling, yet we had more to overcome than nerves. There was no way Pakistan would allow a rag-tag team from Afghanistan to beat them. It would be shameful. The hosts would do everything to prevent our unlikely triumph. It felt like the referee was biased and the team we were playing against was permitted to draft in new players for the final.

For 30 minutes we played well. We tried, we pushed and probed, but when they scored the opening goal any hope we had vanished quicker than the air from our lungs. We fumed at the referee, who had ignored the obvious handball; the goal clearly should not have been allowed. We didn't know how to lift ourselves out of the feeling that the result had been predetermined. We were angry and hurt and we fell apart. We lost 3–0.

'Shit,' said Maryam.

We all sat in the centre circle as the winning team were awarded the small plastic trophy. We had played well; we had given a good account of ourselves. We had had chances to win, but it was as if the ball was always bouncing a few inches from where we needed it to be. I had believed we would win, up until the moment the final whistle blew.

'The referee, though,' said one of the girls.

I nodded. The referee was Pakistani, and the hosts of the tournament hadn't expected the little team from Afghanistan to progress.

Then it was our turn to pick up the second-place trophy, but they hadn't expected us to come in the top three, so they presented us with the smaller third-place trophy and we received the prize money allocated to the third-placed team.

We hadn't won, but we hadn't really lost either. We had brought home the first football trophy since the fall of the Taliban. Against the odds, we women had achieved, even though we were unsupported and sometimes actively opposed, and the relatively pampered men's team had failed. They had brought embarrassment to our country and we had brought pride. Everything that had been said about us had been proven wrong, and attitudes towards us were changing.

We were invited to the Afghanistan Embassy for a celebration, where we were fed luxuriously and showered with flowers and gifts. In those moments we forgot about the challenges that were awaiting us back home. We were living in the moment. We had come second. We had come here together and made history. All I could think of was how much Dahmina and Samira would have loved it. How much they deserved to be there.

We had shown that women could and should represent Afghanistan. That is why our defeat felt like a victory, because while the football match mattered, it was about so much more than the game. We were flown back in style: the government paid for us to fly on a chartered plane. It was a world so far removed from the one we knew. We didn't even enter the airport through the main entrance, but were instead whisked through the back and skipped the security queues. Once we were back in Kabul, we were invited to the palace of the president and were photographed with him for the newspapers.

The next day, after our celebrations at the presidential palace, we had a scheduled team meeting, and that was the moment we realised that half the team were gone.

8

You have to learn to win as a team and lose as a team. If someone makes a mistake, you have to help them forget it immediately. You can't play if you're afraid of making a mistake. You'll never do anything good. Open your eyes.

Our hope had lasted barely a day. In that first meeting after our 2007 tour to Pakistan we realised our teammates weren't just running late. They weren't going to attend at all. Their families had come under pressure from distant relatives and the wider community, who disapproved of them allowing their daughters to play football. They were called names. Their fathers and brothers were shamed for allowing the girls to dishonour their families. It wasn't a group of men stabbing our ball with a knife this time, but the message and the threat were the same. We all knew what could happen to women and girls who dishonoured their families. And so, the flame of joy and hope we had felt as a team was quickly extinguished by the reality of our circumstances, and the fear of the potential repercussions.

Those of us who remained hoped things would be better. We hoped that things would be different after our performance in Pakistan. After all, we had managed to gain assurances from President Karzai that he would help us find a better place than the tennis court to train. After all, hadn't we proved that we deserved their support? We were told that our new 'pitch' and practice location would be in the Nato/ISAF compound. The International Security Assistance Force was a multinational military mission of Nato which was supposed to train the Afghan National Security Forces, help secure Kabul and facilitate the formation of a new government led by Karzai.

When we got there, we realised that there was no football pitch in the Nato/ISAF compound. Since it was the centre point of the new government's military operations, it was also one of the most highly targeted areas in Kabul for the Taliban and other insurgent organisations. The 'football pitch' we had been promised was no more than a patch of green space where army planes would land, along with any US or Nato planes. Despite the Afghanistan NOC's brand-new football stadium sitting empty only a few miles away, this was what we were being offered – or, more aptly, relegated to. We were naive to a certain extent. Ultimately, we were being used by the government to show how things were changing and how much more progressive Afghanistan was becoming after the fall of the Taliban. But it was a veneer. Surface-level support. Our day-to-day reality, we would quickly learn, would not change.

On top of this we had to deal with those who didn't believe we should be playing at all. Street harassment was vicious for all of us. On the way to training sessions we were regularly the targets of abuse. Comments were fired at us relentlessly.

Maryam and I were walking back from training one day when a man recognised us from the international news coverage. He began to follow us down the road, shouting awful accusations at us: we were non-Islamic, we were westernised, we were prostitutes. He would not give up. We ignored him and kept our heads down, waiting for him to lose interest, but he didn't stop pounding down the street closely behind us, peppering us with insults. Eventually, when he failed to provoke a response, he leapt towards me, grabbed my bum and thrust his hands over my body. I felt so violated. Shocked by the sudden invasive breach of my personal space, the unsolicited invasion of my body, I felt myself switch. Rage erupted up and out of me.

I quickly snatched up my large Adidas bag that had fallen to the floor and began swinging it at him, into him. It was loaded with all my training gear, my boots, my laptop, a two-litre bottle of water. I knew that it was heavy. I beat him with my bag in one hand and with my other hand clenched into a fist, pummelling wherever I could reach him. Through the red mist that had descended over me I could tell he was surprised by my reaction. Women in Afghanistan do not retaliate against men, whether it be with a look, their body language or verbally, let alone by physically fighting back. In our society, this is not acceptable. If a woman is being beaten it is because she deserved it or earned it. But I was sick of it. I was sick and tired of being walked over and abused just for being a woman. And so, I let go. I did everything I could to protect myself. I felt an energy rear up inside of me, like a lioness charging full speed to protect herself.

I had him on the ground and I kept attacking him. Two decades of oppression were spilling out of me, onto a man who – in that moment – embodied all of the men who had ever wronged me, taken away what I loved or pushed the heel of oppression down on my sisters. I wanted to kill him. I was scaring myself. I felt Maryam pulling my shoulders away and trying to push me through the crowd that had gathered to watch what was happening. Except she wasn't strong enough. I shrugged free of her and kept kicking at the body of the man who had grabbed me. He pulled himself onto his knees gingerly and up onto his feet, but before he could try and move away someone in the crowd grabbed him and pushed his face towards me: 'Beat him,' he instructed me. I did, continuously. It was wrong, an overspilling of emotions that went way too far. Eventually the mist lifted and Maryam dragged me away, adrenaline washing away to be replaced by shame as the man lay bleeding on the ground.

'Don't,' she said. 'Don't give them a reason to say this is what playing football does to us.'

I knew she was right, but the anger came from so many places, including how my family were being mistreated and targeted. My mum had her judgement questioned daily, both inside and outside of school, and the pressure was intense. Unlike me, my mum didn't fight back. She doesn't like confrontation and she has always been respectful and polite. She has a kind nature and because of this she would fall victim to their torment. Any conflict I was dragged into she would also be involved in, and it was very difficult for her. If any teachers or the headteacher had a problem with me they would go to my mum, expecting her to punish me and bring me in line. She just calmly absorbed their pressure, their judgement and comments, but later, when she came home, she would cry. I hated to see that. I wanted her to defend herself, to tell them if they had a problem with me they needed to speak to me, to tell them that when we enter the school gates she is a teacher and not my mother. But she didn't. Instead, she would come home, sit with my dad and cry. I could see how much it hurt and frustrated her. She didn't fight those people, but she never once told me to stop what I was doing, and that might have been her own way of pushing back. Even though I felt selfish and guilty, I was never going to give in and let them win, otherwise it all would have been for nothing. So we swallowed it all.

Maryam and I never spoke of what happened that day in the street. My mother shielded us from the extent of what was said to her. We took the anger and the hate and we buried it within us.

My brothers faced similar treatment. They would return home with bloody noses or mouths because they had fought back when someone at school called me names, insulted our family's integrity or told them they needed to go and put on a burqa because they were not real men – for allowing me to play football. They didn't want to go back to school; they were frustrated by the constant attention and embarrassed. They were young teenagers and didn't understand what was happening and why it was happening.

My dad was defensive, bold, outspoken and headstrong like myself. He would challenge anyone who questioned my actions and blamed him for what they deemed immoral: 'She is my daughter. I am responsible. I have given her this freedom. She's not on your payroll, she's not taking the money from you. She's not living in your home. It's not your responsibility, so why are you talking or judging or questioning? It's not your business. This is my daughter, and I will let her to do whatever she wants.'

And if it was this bad for me, I knew it would be so much worse for the others. I could not blame those who walked away, or those who had taken advantage of new connections they had made as a result of being part of the team to find a way out of the country on scholarships.

'Off, off, off,' the Nato soldier shouted, waving at us as he ran onto the grass. Dutifully, we each picked up the nearest cone to us and ran as fast as we could to the side. We watched as a single lonely cone was blown sideways by the downdraught of a huge helicopter coming in to land. We sat in any shade we could find, the scalding air blowing in our faces. The soldiers ran to and fro. There was no way of knowing how long this would take.

I realised that we had been set up for failure from the very beginning. But we had succeeded anyway, so now, while the Football Federation couldn't actively shut us down, they were trying to force us out by making our training sessions as dangerous as humanly possible for us. We didn't question it though; we were just grateful for the crumbs from the table and would take any opportunity that came our way. We treated every small opportunity as a big one. Living in Afghanistan as women was dangerous as it was and we were already risking our lives by playing football. We weren't going to be put off by the increased risk of training in the compound. Why didn't we say no and ask for more or better? Because we didn't want to risk losing what was on offer. We could have demanded a safer location, away from the place that was most targeted by terrorists at that time, but we didn't want to run the risk of being sent back to the tennis court or of having even that taken away from us for being ungrateful. So we made our peace with the helicopters.

To get into the compound we had to pass through military checkpoints, past armed soldiers who didn't want us there. There were always explosions around that area and the threat of attack hung in the air constantly. The only way of getting to and from the area, other than by foot, was via taxi, but we were all students and financially dependent on our parents, so we couldn't afford them. We would walk for miles after school, with our big bags containing our books, kit and training equipment, to get there for 2 p.m., by which time the sun was high in the sky at its strongest, beating down on us painfully as we played. We would always arrive tired and hungry, and desperate to get started. We would get no prior warning of delays, because it was a security risk to disclose that information. So, we would pull out our ball and start passing it about until the whirring of a helicopter getting louder would force us to clear to the side. Sometimes I was coaching and laying out plastic cones and the incoming helicopter would send them spinning away into the air.

We couldn't speak to the soldiers. They were allowed to shoot anyone they felt threatened by, so we couldn't risk it. We would just have to leave when the time was up, training or no training. One day, when I was thoroughly pissed off by the relentless challenges, I paused to look at a painting on the wall, street art of a woman's eyes, next to where an American soldier was standing. I was hot and sweaty, and my hair clung to my forehead. There was nowhere for us to wash after training, and we had to leave in the searing afternoon heat, with the stench of our efforts potent and uncomfortable. The image on the wall distracted me from that discomfort though. I wanted to take a photo of it and so I pulled my phone from my pocket and pointed the camera towards the wall.

I felt the sudden push of cold metal against my head. The soldier had panicked and, moving quickly, he launched the end of his gun towards my face, pressing the end of the barrel into my temple.

'What the fuck are you doing?' I said. 'Is there a threat towards your life here?'

I was shocked, scared and angry. Yes, I was standing outside the Nato/ISAF compound, but I was far from being a threat. I stood there gripping my phone, frozen. He hadn't expected me to speak English, and I could tell that I had taken him by surprise. It was obviously nothing compared to the shock I felt, but I had angered him now.

'Stay still or I'll blow your brains out,' he proffered menacingly.

'Listen, you came to my country to protect us, not to blow our heads off,' I reasoned. 'Why the fuck did you come to our country if you don't know what you're here for? I'm not a threat to you. I don't have anything on me, any gun, any weapons. I'm a civilian and you are holding a gun to my head, unprovoked.'

'I am authorised to take whatever action I deem necessary if I feel threatened,' he replied, deadpan.

He was right, of course. It wouldn't be hard for him to justify his actions, because he only needed his word against mine. And if I wasn't there to give my word, how could anyone prove I wasn't threatening him? He was supposed to be here to help us against the Taliban, but here he was, just another man threatening a woman.

'My parents tell me this country is my home, but if I can't feel safe in my home where can I?'

I was playing with fire, but I felt the pressure on my head ease slightly. Although I had bitten back, my bolshiness had worked in my favour this time, disarming him metaphorically and literally. I grabbed the holdall I had dropped to the floor and hurried away without looking back, leaping on the small window of opportunity to remove myself.

★

We started to recruit and rebuild the team again, going from school to school, with footballs purchased with our pocket money. We volunteered in tournaments and festivals and continued to build our network.

We found Jamila, a new left back from a school in the north of the city, who we nicknamed Roberto Carlos because of how hard she kicked the ball. We needed an entire new centre midfield, as both players had been forced to quit after Pakistan. That was solved by Esini and Hajira, two best friends who hardly spoke to anyone at training but never stopped running.

The core of us who remained were passionately invested in the development of women's football and the national team. We were willing to continue despite the increased risks. But I realised that in order to protect myself I couldn't become too attached. I knew any one of our teammates could be taken away at any moment. I couldn't let my heart be broken every time it happened, or I wouldn't be able to keep going. And I was determined to make real change.

I started to challenge the Football Federation more. When our team was asked to go and welcome the men's national team at the airport, I protested: 'Why? We're not their cheerleaders. We may not be considered professionals as they are, but we have the title of national team players and that deserves respect. We won't go to the airport and stand there with flowers to welcome the men's team home. Don't insult us.'

It felt as if every part of my life involved a fight, and the more I fought, the more opposition I faced from all sides. I began studying for my degree. My mother often found me asleep at my desk, exhausted, my face resting on a textbook.

Despite my hard work, a lecturer at my university threatened to fail me in his class. 'No matter what happens,' he said, smirking, 'you will be failed. You cannot graduate from the university without passing my class and I will never let you to do that.' He stood with his face close to mine, his black eyes boring down at me spitefully, unable to mask how much he was enjoying this. He wanted to crush my resolve. He was trying to intimidate me. He didn't like that I asked questions; he didn't like my sporty clothes or the way I wore my scarf – which I always wore, but casually, thrown half-heartedly around my neck, which seemed to unintentionally provoke him.

He constantly tried to scare me by weaponising religion, because in Afghanistan non-belief or being seen to be undermining religion can get you killed. He assumed I was religious, because everyone was, and he believed the threats would be effective as a result. He threatened me with the wrath of God, highlighting God's power over me and my life. Yet, the decision of whether to pass me or not in this class was not God's decision, it was his. He was aware of his power and he was using it against me.

When I challenged him on this and asked him explicitly the true reasons for failing me, he said: 'To begin with, I hate your outfit. Secondly, you are asking too many questions; you do not know your place. And, thirdly, you are promoting a non-religious culture, which is unacceptable. You will never pass your exams. Ever. No matter what you do, you will fail. Either I will resign from school or I will force you out.'

I started to panic. I had this lecturer for two semesters and I needed to pass his classes or I would fail my degree. Under his hateful gaze, I felt myself shrinking into the corridor floor. I was used to insults and abuse, but someone actively threatening my studies – someone who had power over the outcome of my situation regardless of how hard I worked – was a whole other ball game. It rocked me. I felt completely lost, but I would never give up that easily.

I knew I couldn't speak to my family because of how worried they would be, so I decided to seek advice from the one person at university that I trusted: a lecturer named Amir, who had been very supportive of me. I strode into his classroom without knocking, fuelled by frustration and anger.

'I don't know what to do,' I said, my mind whirring through the limited options available to me. 'I need to pass. I need to get my degree but I can't do it because of this lecturer. He's threatened to fail me regardless of what I do,' I explained.

Amir listened patiently, until I finally stopped speaking and sat down, with my head in my hands. 'Go and change your entire outfit,' he said gently. He looked slightly amused by the dumbfounded expression on my face.

Compliance did not come naturally to me, especially when I disagreed with something. In fact, it was never even a consideration for me; I never contemplated it. This was a new lesson I had to learn: that sometimes, we have to play the game – even if the rules are rigged – in order to win. Playing by their rules, if you have to, does not mean accepting defeat if you have a long-term strategy.

'On those days when you have his classes, cover yourself from top to toe,' Amir clarified.

Still, I felt resistant to the idea, sceptical that it would work and resentful that I had to pretend to be something other than myself.

'Tell him that you regret your actions and behaviour so much, that you have converted to Islam. Show him that you now hate everything about the way you used to live your life. You are now working to correct yourself, as you have seen the light and want to be a good Muslim girl. I, in turn, will confirm this. I will tell him that I have started mentoring you and that you have totally changed your life around.'

I hated the idea, but it made sense. There would be no other way of convincing the overzealous lecturer. I needed to bypass him and to do this I needed to conform. Ultimately, I decided, that would be the bigger win. So that is what I did.

I prepared myself and within days I stood in a toilet cubicle, pulling a long dress down over myself. I swore profusely as I tried to pin my scarf more neatly around my head, tucking the stray and wild wisps of hair beneath the material over and over until they were mostly invisible. I paused, and looked at myself in the mirror despairingly. I always had a very difficult time hiding my authentic self. I hated looking at a version of myself that felt like a lie, but I was motivated by the bigger picture. This was just another challenge, another match to win, and I was determined to succeed.

As I promised Amir, I apologised to the other lecturer. I channelled the demeanour of every submissive Afghan woman I could think of. I avoided eye contact, kept my gaze fixed to the floor, and my voice quiet, unassuming.

'I am sorry professor,' I said quietly. 'I am stupid and confused. I have lost my way. I have been having regular sessions with another professor to correct my behaviour. If there is anything I can learn from you too about what it means to be a good Muslim woman I would be very grateful for your wisdom.'

Inside, I was almost screaming with a sort of maniacal delirious laughter: I had training at two o'clock, where my rebellion against every word I was uttering was already lined up. Strangely, playing this role – the very opposite of what I was, the very thing Afghanistan society wanted me to be – empowered me. I was in control: acting, playing a game, a game that I would win.

The lecturer believed me. Of course he did. Of course he believed that he had forced me into submission, because women were weak and submissive, it was innate. But every time I left his class to secretly go to training, I would tear the costume off and put on the clothes I felt most comfortable in – my football kit.

I spent as little time around that lecturer as possible. So much so that I skipped my graduation. I placed no importance on the ceremony because I wasn't interested in wearing my disguise and celebrating in a room of my oppressors, men who had tried to break my character. Instead, I collected my degree certificate a few days later. I felt deep down that I had won a small battle, not only against the tyranny of one man holding far more power than he should have, but over myself, because I had learnt to achieve my goals by fighting back in a quieter, more transgressive way. I was fatigued, but I had made it to the finish line, and I was ready for the next challenge.

9

When you are on the pitch, you have to imagine what your opponent is going to do, what your teammate will do. You have to constantly adapt and change, mixing instinct with practice, imagination with knowledge. To be part of a team in these moments is to feel fully alive, fully human. Open your eyes.

'Khalida.'

Maryam's voice was hushed at the other end of the phone.

'The women have left.'

The phone ringing had been a loud disruption in my quiet hotel room, and it startled me. I thanked her and put the phone down.

It was 2010 and we had travelled to Germany again, this time with the whole team, for a training camp. But when we had arrived at the airport in Kabul, two of my teammates' names were missing from the list. In their places were two names I didn't know. When they arrived it took me a while to work out where I recognised them from. And then it hit me: they had attended a coaching course, but had never played for the team. The others were equally confused. What was going on? The women who had been left behind were not only two of our best players, but also two of the strongest personalities, and integral to the functioning of our team. They had been replaced by two young women who were effectively strangers to us.

They stood quietly to the side, their heads bowed, avoiding eye contact. They were a very different profile of player to the rest of us. They were not athletes – you could tell from their build and mannerisms. We had dominant characters that were physical and athletic and not very feminine, and they were the opposite. No one said anything to them. We were wary of them. We saw them as part of the problem, and we blamed them for the absence of our teammates. On reflection, it was unfair.

'Ummm, who are they?' whispered Maryam to me.

We found out that an Afghan coach who had links in Europe had invited these two women to join the group. I was frustrated that two good players had been removed without our knowledge, but in addition to that, something just felt wrong. Who were these women? Why and how had they been invited? Why was our coach so friendly with them? I made sure that the two new women shared a room with Maryam and I told her to pay attention to them, to report back anything suspicious: where they went, who they saw.

As captain, when we were travelling I would often speak to my teammates between rooms on the hotel room phones. They trusted me. If there was a problem, they would call me or come and find me. That trust had been built up over months, over years. The shared rebellion of playing football had bonded us together and they respected the sacrifices I made for the sake of the team.

On the first night, the phone rang. The two women had gone and no one knew where.

'OK,' I said. 'Just try and find out where they are, Maryam.'

'We can't find them,' she whispered. 'They've disappeared.'

'OK,' I said. 'Let's see what happens when they come back: how they are and how they behave. We need to try and work out their situation. Just pay attention, don't sleep until they come back to the room.'

The hotel was part of a sports complex. It was far from the city centre and there was nowhere to go nearby. Nowhere to hang out or visit. I started phoning around the various rooms I knew players were in to ask if the women were there. As each reply came back negative, my curiosity peaked and I became concerned. I decided to go and check the coaches' rooms.

Striding confidently down the corridor, I paused outside the room where the Afghan coach was staying. I knocked tentatively. I could hear voices on the other side of the door. He swung it open and looked sheepishly at me. Behind him, one of the women was sprawled on the bed and another was lying on the sofa. He laughed, noticing my reaction when I saw them in his room. 'Oh, they had to talk to me about something,' he said, 'that's why they are in my room.'

I could see what was happening. The one on the bed was clutching a glass; the other had one nearby on a table, next to a box of half-eaten chocolates. I could smell alcohol in the air and see it in their behaviour.

'I know what is happening here,' I said.

He had stepped backwards, and I walked into his room and picked up a chocolate.

'I love chocolate!' I exclaimed.

'Hey, don't, it has alcohol in it,' he said, gesturing for me not to eat it.

'Why are you giving them alcoholic chocolates and drinks? They are athletes. We are here to train.'

'They wanted to try it; it's just a taste.'

He was casual in his response, but I wasn't stupid.

'I know what is happening, I'm not a child,' I said. I looked at the two women and I could see the colour draining from their faces as panic set in. In Afghanistan, being found in a man's bedroom would be incredibly dangerous for a woman. On top of that, they were consuming alcohol, which is illegal in Afghanistan. They didn't say anything; they just looked at the coach. But he said nothing either. I turned and left.

Back in my room I went into the bathroom for some privacy and sat on the lid of the toilet. I felt shaky. I didn't know how to help these women. They had clearly been brought to Germany for exactly this reason. They were young, vulnerable teenagers. They had been promised a trip abroad and manipulated.

'This is such bullshit,' said Maryam. 'They can't get away with this.'

The next day, they disappeared again. I was scared for them, but I was angry too, angry that coaches were taking advantage of our platform for their own gains, using our sacrifices. This time more of us looked for the two women, but they were nowhere to be found. They weren't in the coach's room, so we tried our playboy coach. He stepped out into the corridor and told us that no one was with him, promising to help look for them. A couple of hours later, he came to tell me that the women had 'gone for a walk'. The look on his face as he spoke suggested that it was ridiculous for him to even be speaking to us about this, as if he was above the situation. It made my blood boil with anger. These men were clearly closing ranks.

Maryam reported back to me that when the two women returned to their room they went straight to the bathroom together, shut themselves in, and took it in turns to shower. It was strange behaviour. At training the following day I watched them closely. I could see a large mark on one woman's neck. They were behaving oddly, keeping their bodies hidden. They constantly pulled their sleeves over their hands. They wore unusually bunched scarves, which was weird, as we didn't wear scarves for training, because there were no men around. They stood together, to the side of the pitch. On one level I didn't want to attack women in any way, but this was the kind of scandal that the Football Federation needed to shut us down. It was everything that those people in the street had whispered about us. I was determined to pull away the cloak of secrecy.

'What happened to your neck?' I asked one of them. It felt brutal just to ask like this, but I needed to know. 'We are in the training camp, there are no men here. We are on your side. What happened to your neck? Why is there a mark there? Where were you last night?'

The women were panicking, their eyes moist. By this point the other players had shifted to face them, also wanting answers. The safeguarding officer, an old woman sent along by the NOC who was close to retirement and had always operated on the fringes of our activities, suddenly walked over.

'She got that mark a long time ago. It's a birthmark, it's not something new,' she interrupted my questioning.

Maryam was furious. 'We are not children!' she cried. 'This mark was not there yesterday. Stop lying to us!'

Our attempt to reach the truth failed. They were too scared to talk. We went on training, with an air of sadness and frustration hanging over us. The same pattern of activity repeated day after day: they vanished, they returned hours later, they hid the new marks as best they could, and they wouldn't tell us what was happening to them. They were always together, always silent.

Eventually I decided that enough was enough. I simply would not stand for it. I confronted one of the coaches. 'We all fought so hard and sacrificed so much,' I said. 'We are not here for this. What is happening in this training camp – what you deny is happening but what we can see with our own eyes – is wrong. It is undermining what we're trying to do and I will not stand here and allow it to continue. I am going to report this to the president of the federation.'

They all banded together out of fear. They threatened us; they accused us of spreading rumours and said the coaches would resign in protest as a result. I was so angry, at the women in particular.

'How dare you? How dare you betray your sisters for the crumbs from these men's table? I hope it's worth it.'

They stayed silent and refused to meet my eyes. They were clearly poisoned by fear, but despite understanding this I still couldn't comprehend how some women could police other women, subjugate them and conform to a male world just to protect themselves. The coaches stopped interacting with the players entirely after that. They hid in their rooms and leapt at any opportunity they had to express how upset they were with the team. They were masters of emotional manipulation, trying to subvert themselves into the true victims of the situation. They were trying to manipulate us, the same way they manipulated and preyed upon their victims.

When we returned to Afghanistan, I immediately went to see Karim. The whole place was filled with armed bodyguards and security; it was more like entering another army compound than a government building. In spite of the fact that I had been a regular visitor to the building for months, I still received curious looks and muttered comments as the men passed me by. 'Come see me after,' catcalled one man as he walked down the corridor, laughing with a colleague.

I had to lay all of that aside as I worked my way towards the red carpeted stairs that led to the Football Federation's offices within the building. There were three main rooms to get through to reach Karim – his secretary's office, a meeting room and then his office – and they were at the far end of the building. I told Karim's secretary that I wanted to speak to him, and he shuffled away to check that I could enter before returning and sitting behind his desk. Karim's booming voice called me in. He was there alone, behind his desk, like a walrus.

'Listen,' I said, before we had even sat down. 'The reason I came here is because of all the bullshit happening in our training camps. We have been forced to take two men with us who were only there to have a good time. They're exploiting our name and our platform, and taking advantage of our opportunities. I want these men away from our team and the two women involved need to be questioned about what happened to them. I want action taken. I'm worried for these women. They were promised a trip to Germany. Of course, they were excited to get out of Afghanistan, it's an amazing opportunity, but what they have had to pay for it is going too far.'

'Whoah, whoah,' said Karim. 'I am just catching up. Start at the beginning. Which women?'

I patiently explained what I had seen on the trip to Germany.

He seemed furious as I spoke. 'This is utterly unacceptable,' he said. 'There will be repercussions for all of these men. They will lose their jobs.'

Karim asked his secretary to call someone and then immediately started tearing him to shreds on the phone while I was there.

'That was the coach.'

Karim's voice became gentle. 'I promise we will fix this,' he assured me. 'But we cannot take this outside of the federation. That would risk destroying all your hard work, all the sacrifice. You will be back at zero and nobody will trust that it is safe for girls to play football.'

I felt excited and relieved as I left his office. Even though everyone knew the rumours about his treatment of women, I thought that perhaps they were not that accurate. I felt like Karim was taking me – and the women's team in general – seriously. But, instead of being fired, the coaches were taken off women's football and given other roles. Essentially, they were promoted. They were moved into different positions, which, for them, was synonymous with being rewarded, as in their eyes there was no lower place to work than women's football. I sucked up this small blow. I didn't care if they were falling upwards, because I was so relieved that they were finally gone from our orbit.

We never saw the two women who came to Germany again. They had no friends on the team, so there was very little we could do.

★

After that Karim was more attentive to the team, inviting us all to his office, telling us to treat him like a father figure and that he saw us all as his daughters. It was the first time he had spoken to us without our coach present. He insulted the male coaches and swore when he spoke about them. 'I will never forgive what happened in Germany and I want to be involved in women's football,' he promised. 'I am invested and I want to make sure that you get the best we can get you.' At one stage his eyes filled with tears as he spoke. We trusted him.

I took advantage of his goodwill to say how wrong it was to have a man coaching the women's team and representing women's football: 'What is he bringing to the table? What does he have that I don't have?' By that time, I had begun my second degree in marketing and business. 'I have the education,' I continued. 'I'm more educated than him. I play football, I'm in women's football. I know how to use a computer, I speak a foreign language. I'm well educated, I have degrees. I have good grades. I have everything that is needed. What I don't have is work experience in an office because I was a teacher.'

I had been teaching in two schools, in a private school and then coaching in one of the football academy schools. From 5 a.m. to 8.30 a.m. I would teach and coach in the academy, and from 9 a.m. to 12.30 p.m. I taught IT in the private primary school. I would then go to university and by 3 p.m. I was at training. It was a vicious and gruelling daily routine. It was impossible for Karim to argue with my credentials as a candidate to take on the role of head of women's football.

'I can represent the team. I can represent us better. I can go and talk on behalf of women's football,' I enthused. 'People can trust me more and it will create a safer environment for players, as their families will know that it's women who are leading things.'

'You have to understand why this can't be,' he said. 'There will be a riot.'

'But just think how good it will look to the outside world,' I countered. 'Especially for the man who is driving this change.'

He still looked unsure, so I played my final and strongest card.

'It will make us far more attractive to foreign investment.'

He continued putting up a fight, but I could see by the look in his eyes that I had him.

Finally, at the end of our lengthy negotiation, I left his office with not one position but two: head of women's football and the federation's finance officer.

10

Football is a game of space. You have to learn to make the pitch big when you attack and small when you defend. But it only works if you all move together. Open your eyes.

'You have to understand, it's not my choice,' said coach Wahidullah, his eyes pleading with me. 'It's the situation I'm in. I can't play you. I'm being put under pressure.' He was sweating, clearly scared. 'They said if I play you there will be a big problem for my family.'

I should have known this would happen. My profile was growing, so of course they needed to take me down.

'We are a team,' I replied. 'I was the one who brought you in as a coach. I trust you and you're working under my watch. I'm a player at heart and I want to play, but I will not put you at risk. I understand that you need this job and the salary to put food on the table for your family, so I would never risk that happening to you. I totally understand. It's nothing.'

I had walked out of Karim's office with the promise of two new jobs dangled in front of me, but it would not be confirmed until I was officially voted in by the members of the Football Federation. So, one morning in December 2009, I found myself standing in the toilet of an unfamiliar hotel, fixing a scarf over my hair and making sure my sleeves were pulled down over my arms. I hadn't told my parents where I was going and I kept my unusually traditional outfit in my bag until I was far from home.

I stared at myself in the mirror, checking for flaws, breathing deeply. I steeled myself, breathed again, and pushed the door open and walked out.

The large function room was already very full of people when I entered, and I could feel every eye in the room searing through my secreting layers, scornful of the inferior being underneath. But I knew I couldn't cower in the corner. As head of the women's football committee I was automatically on the board and so I was expected at the top table. I had to walk down the middle of the room proudly. I placed one foot in front of the other, and kept my shoulders back and my head high.

Karim was at the head table. In Kabul, the Football Federation was part of the more conservative and oppressive elements of the city, but the footballing leaders from the provinces made those men look like progressives in comparison. No woman had ever worked for the federation and here I was, being put straight into a position of power. They looked at me with a mixture of astonishment, horror and naked curiosity. Perhaps the presence of FIFA representatives should have made me feel more secure, but it did little to quell the mixture of lecherousness, shock and disdain that was aimed towards me from all angles.

I would later learn that, for whatever reason, Karim hadn't told the federation's representatives of his plan for me to take on the role of finance officer. However, inside the room, his endorsement was clear, as representative after representative went over to have urgent conversations with him. Some came away shaking their heads and looking at me. In the end, when the ballots were counted, with FIFA observers watching, I was elected. There was little fanfare, because no one would stand against Karim's recommended candidate, but as the conference dispersed and I walked back through the room I felt not-so-subtle hands against my body, and I writhed and wriggled away from the chubby fingers of those who wanted to remind me of where I stood. Some grasped my hand to shake it and congratulate me on my new roles, but the applause could not have felt less sincere. Some were flirtatious and tried to get my number, others brushed close against me as they passed, and yet more were openly hostile.

The next day I walked into the office to start a job no one wanted me to have. In not telling anyone that he had appointed me, Karim caused conflict amongst many of the people working there, but it was I who was in the centre of the storm rather than him. The former finance officer was friends with our former coach and they both had plenty of allies in the federation. In their eyes, I had usurped their roles. Their hatred – and the hatred of their allies – towards me was palpable. They thought that I was surely having an affair with Karim, as that was the only explanation they could find for my elevation at their expense.

I decided to ignore the general feeling around me and throw myself head first into the job. The first thing I did was to hire a new coach, who I had met on a coaching course. I knew he was a good man who was genuinely interested in women's football. Then I reached out to every contact at every NGO, charity and football association I had ever been in touch with. I asked for help; I cold-called and emailed anyone who might be able to help grow football. We needed money and we needed expertise.

I felt like I was living some sort of dream. I was able to give up the teaching and I had been given power that enabled me to grow women's football and support the players. But, at the same time, it was a bittersweet venture: I was the only woman who had ever worked in any position of power there, and it showed. The corridors reeked of cigarettes, body odour and chauvinism. My colleagues would abandon the table I sat down at to eat my lunch. They would leave rooms when I entered and refused to talk to me. If I attended meetings, they would make crude jokes and find ways to undermine my intelligence. In one of the first meetings I attended, a junior member of staff asked me whether

I knew what four plus four was, getting a laugh from everyone in the room. I had to go to the toilets and breathe deeply to control my emotions.

My parents still believed that I was teaching and running from place to place. They were worried about me, because I was sleeping very little and studying late into the night to complete my second degree. Again, my mum would often find me face down, asleep on my books. They worried about my mental health and well-being. I didn't tell them where I was working, because I was scared. I knew they would try and stop me. Everyone knew the reputation of the federation, they knew that no women worked there beyond cleaners or cooks, and they understood what kind of working environment existed there. Yet, I believed I was there to change things, to be a voice for women in the decision-making process, to challenge the system and ensure that women's football was a safe space. I felt like I needed to be a part of things to be able to do that.

One evening, I returned home to find my mother and father sitting at the kitchen table waiting for me, their faces hard. 'Khalida, do not lie to us. We have seen the news. Your photo is everywhere. What is going on?'

That was how I learnt that my appointment had been announced on TV and in the media. It was huge news. I had no idea. My image was everywhere: photos of me sitting on the top table amid a sea of hulking old men.

'Yes, I have taken the job at the Football Federation. It is the only way that women will truly be supported,' I said.

My mother just looked at me, shaking her head. 'Khalida, I have always supported you,' she said. 'Perhaps too much. But this? You are painting a target on your back. It is too dangerous.'

'That's exactly why I have to do it. I know the risks and I know there will be a price to pay, but you raised me to value my voice, to protect others who cannot look after themselves. I couldn't live with myself if I hid from this.'

My father looked more worried than angry. 'This is the most dangerous thing you have ever done.' He paused and lowered his voice slightly. 'Karim is a dangerous man. I have told you before. You know about his reputation. We cannot protect you from this.'

'You brought us back to Afghanistan. You wanted us to connect with our home. Well, I stood on that pitch in Pakistan and I wept as I sang the national anthem. This is how I am honouring my home. I am trying to make it a better place for everyone, to build a better future.'

At that, my mother stood up. 'I cannot speak to her anymore,' she said, and without looking at me, she left the room.

Even Idris stopped speaking to me for a while because my mum was so upset. My quiet, gentle brother, who would always come and talk to me, asking my opinion on anything and everything, asking for my advice on everything he did, now saw me as an antagonist. He blamed me for needlessly upsetting our mother. It broke my heart. But I knew he was too young to understand.

The media interest in my appointment gave me a small window of power. As finance officer, I was responsible for all the federation employees' wages, which were paid in person. Each month they would have to come and collect their pay. But they refused.

'It's against our honour to take our salary from a woman,' they argued. 'We don't talk to her. Why would we go and take our salary from her? It's against our religion and damaging to our reputation.'

The first month, they refused their salaries and only a few people came to collect their wages. The rest tried to send people on their behalf, but I stood firm and refused: 'This is not a restaurant or cafe where you can order coffee and send a friend up to collect it.' I was determined that even if I only lasted a couple of months, I wasn't going to back down.

I suspected that Karim putting me in charge of the federation's finances was a tactical move on his part. He had become weary and frustrated with men in the position. Corruption was rife. It was normalised and ran through the federation at every level. Karim was not trying to prevent corruption; he just wanted to control it. Having a woman in charge was his answer. He believed that no woman would dare steal from the federation and that a woman could be easily manipulated to be on his side and play by his rules. He also clearly thought I could be bought, that handing me positions of power meant I was under his control and that I would trade my morals for career progression. Equally, it set me up for failure. If money went missing, I could be blamed and I was expendable; it was a quick and easy way to drive me out if he needed to. He could manipulate the situation to suit his needs. It would be far harder for him to undermine my position as head of women's football, but there were many ways my finance role offered ways to entrap me.

It was a risk to name me head of the women's football committee, and Karim was well aware of this. I was qualified, but problematic: I was bold, outspoken and lacked the modesty expected of my gender. Operating outside the federation I had been a constant thorn in their side. Karim wanted to reduce the impact of my voice, but first he had to make me seem like one of them. I was blind to what was happening.

I warned the vice president to pass on a message to Karim: 'Go give this message to the president. Tell him that I've made this announcement to all employees: there is no salary if you do not respect me. If you do not come and stand in front of my desk with respect and accept who I am, then no wages will be paid. This is my position. There's no other way.'

I also warned that if there was any attempt to bypass me on this issue, then I would resign immediately and go straight to the press. I had a window, a small window of time during which the reputation of the federation would have been severely damaged if I left so soon after being appointed, and I was taking advantage of it. Hiring the first woman to work at the federation was a big story, but I knew an immediate resignation would be a bigger one. 'If the president interferes,' I announced, 'I won't just resign, I'll resign in public and I will tell them everything: every detail about my experience here.'

It was important to establish myself and gain their respect. If I just handed the wages over to their go-betweens, then I would not be respecting my own position. The entire intention and purpose of the sacrifice, of my reputation in working there, and the risk I was taking was to make the position of women stronger and change people's mindsets. If I just accepted their resistance, I would be doing the opposite and confirming their prejudicial views on women.

Some employees backed down, but four still refused to enter my office, a space I had been given – despite the rest of the workplace being open plan – because everyone refused to work near me. I waited them out and, eventually, one by one, they came to collect their money. One employee stubbornly went without his wages for four whole months before he finally relented and skulked through the door, staring at me aggressively as he collected the back pay he could no longer do without.

I was responsible for paying expenses too. Some of the men would come with inflated bills or invoices. They expected that I wouldn't know the true cost of things and would just hand over any amount of money they requested. Instead, I paid attention to every minute detail, so I wouldn't make a single mistake. I did everything possible to be aware, to be on my toes, and to make sure that I was doing the right thing. Just as I had studied excessively to ensure no one had an excuse to stop me playing football in school, I made sure there was no way I could be penalised for missing money.

Two employees once came to me with e-receipts for petrol, to cover the cost of travel to a football match, but when I did the calculation I could see that the price didn't align with the distance and the cost of fuel. 'This is not correct. The price of the fuel is not the price that you actually bought it at. Where did you buy this from?' They looked at me first, then at each other. 'Either you call the man at the petrol station or I'm going to go there myself and make sure that this is actually the correct receipt, because this price,' I indicated to the receipts they'd brought to me, 'is not right. Why are you trying to steal money? There is only ten extra afghani there. Why would you destroy your reputation for so little money?' I wasn't scared of calling them out or confronting people. Sometimes the men I challenged were more senior than I was.

Karim installed a camera in front of my desk and could see everything that happened. He told me he'd had it installed to both protect me and monitor me, to make sure I wasn't stealing. I missed the point and snapped that he could put a hundred cameras around me, I wasn't going to do anything wrong. I wasn't scared of him watching me. I had nothing to hide.

Every time I looked up, though, I could see his large camera focused on me. Always. It made me feel extremely uncomfortable, but it did give me a layer of protection. I was grateful for it when a coach came in and told me he wanted to coach the women's team to 'take care of the players and their bodies.' Then he said he would be my 'assistant' and 'provide' whenever I wanted a 'massage'. At that moment, all of the anger I had pushed down, from every comment and every look in that building, detonated at once. I grabbed a stone penholder and lobbed it hard towards his face. It flew straight through the large window, with a loud boom. It sounded like an explosion. People came running to my office and asked what had happened.

'This motherfucker,' I said bluntly, and I repeated verbatim what he had said to me.

After that, I decided I wasn't going to be polite and smile and take it any more. I was going to speak the same language as the men around me. I rescinded my shyness. I swore, I raged and I shocked them with my boisterousness. Karim banished that particular coach from the building, but I could see that he enjoyed it. For him it was a game, a form of entertainment. Sitting alone in his office he would pull my face up on his big TV, and he would listen in and laugh.

I knew that the entire culture inside the building needed to change and I was the only person willing to orchestrate it. After I appointed a new coach, I started hiring some of the women's national team players to fill roles within the federation, and I worked with schools and universities to arrange scholarships for players. These two strategies were essential, because the primary challenge for all our players was financial support. They were extremely dedicated and would walk for hours after school to make it to training, because most of them couldn't afford taxis or even the bus. In moments of desperation, some would risk flirting with a taxi driver in exchange for a lift to training, but that was an extremely dangerous thing to do. Many of them also played on empty stomachs, unable to afford food. I explained this to Karim. I highlighted that if one of the players was kidnapped or raped on the way to school or training, it would be hugely problematic and damaging for the federation. I was learning to speak their language.

The players got a small subsidy from the government, but nothing from the federation, and it wasn't enough to survive on. There was lots of money coming in, but we had bargained it away to be allowed to play. Now we needed something back. It didn't eventually come from that pot, which was technically meant for us; instead, it came from international organisations and NGOs that I had made contact with. Through this I had been able to unlock funding to support women's sport in the country.

Though Karim had always been supportive, and it was rare that he turned down one of my requests, I was starting to feel uneasy about him. As we hired more and more women, and even recruited them into more senior positions, the positive news stories flowed. I could see there was benefit for him as the leader of an organisation that could be shown off as evidence of our progress. But there was something about him – the way he spoke to the players, the way his eyes flicked over us – that made me feel very uncomfortable. Yet, I ignored it, seeing it as the price we paid for making real change.

Soon we had five women working in the building in salaried posts. Meanwhile, I had convinced Karim that the federation should provide a small monthly salary to all players. It was 100 US dollars a month for national team players and 50 US dollars for youth team players. That was hugely impactful, because it gave the players power at home. They were earning money from playing, and contributing to family incomes. It was a lot: 100 US dollars was equivalent to around 5,000 to 6,000 afghani – more than many of their fathers and mothers earned a month. Instead of taking from the family purse, they were giving back to it, and that was hugely empowering. This came alongside scholarships, coaching courses and refereeing courses. Meanwhile, a group of schoolteachers who supported the work also got paid for their services. After a lot of negotiating, football for women was becoming not attractive, but tolerable.

I was always tactical. I would never talk about gender, inequality, inhumanity or discrimination, because I knew Karim didn't care, that it was a dead end. Instead, I put my efforts into finding ways to present how it would benefit him personally, how it would be reported, how it would make him look. I was selling him a product that I made him believe he needed to help him extend his power and influence.

When I was told, 'You don't have a budget. Go find yourself a sponsor,' I did. I wrote to every company I could think of, and I searched for the contact details of brand after brand. Hummel, a Danish sportswear manufacturer, was one of the few companies who responded, and they said they would love to support the team. That was the first time a real sponsor entered Afghanistan, and they supported not only women but also the men's team. I had managed to get them to sponsor and manufacture the kits and training gear of the men's, women's and youth teams.

One night, when I was at home, my phone rang. When I answered, I could hear sobbing.

'Khalida, Khalida, you have to help. They've arrested Maryam.'

Maryam had always raged openly at the idea of a former military man rather than a footballer running football. She'd even been vocal about her views in interviews, and that had attracted Karim's attention. She had a part-time job, working as an interpreter for an Australian journalist. We were still as thick as thieves and took risks together.

Her arrest came as a shock. It turned out she had been followed and watched. One day she invited a man into her home for food, while her mum was cooking and her sister was present, but her father was not there. Rumours that she was having an affair with this man had been spread like wildfire. Shortly after he entered their house, those watching called the police, who came and arrested her, along with her sister and mother.

I was terrified. The rose-tinted glasses of trust that Karim had placed over my eyes was ripped off as soon as I heard that handcuffs had been placed on my teammate. I appealed for her freedom, and I begged Karim to help get her and her relatives out of prison. I asked others in the office to help post bail so that we could get them out.

Having never stepped foot in a prison before, I visited Maryam daily. When I entered the prison, I was harassed by the guards, who invited me to sleep with them in exchange for their help in getting my friend and her family out. I kept scanning around for the nearest exit, conscious of needing an escape route should

I be prevented from leaving. There were no rules or laws, and it was feasible that I could end up inside not having committed any crime. Maryam and her family were in a temporary detention centre in the centre of the city, a stone's throw away from the palace where the president of Afghanistan lived. Maryam was cramped into a two-room multiple occupancy cell. It was dark and there were two little windows and a toilet. The floor was soaked, and women and children filled the rooms. I was so used to her as my loud teammate, my friend with her vicious sense of humour, doing impressions of the male coaches, railing against the system. But she had been utterly crushed; the colour had drained out of her. I tried to find that spark within her and light it by telling her we would fight and we would win, like a team, but she just shook her head and faced the wall.

I started talking to other women who were in that prison, and what I heard appalled me. One woman and her small child had been arrested because her husband, who had supported the Taliban, had escaped from custody. Another young woman was in there for having attempted to escape from a forced marriage. Their stories were like the ones I heard from the women and girls who came to training. Their lives were all bound to and at the mercy of men. Here, listening to the women in the prison, I could see it was the same all over the country. And if this was the reality in the city, I wondered what it must be like out in the rural areas. Meanwhile, men like Karim were reaping the benefits of being seen as champions of women's rights and opportunities, whilst so many women were put where nobody could hear their voices.

Every time I walked through the gates I was gripped with fear, but I was their only hope of getting out and I worked tirelessly to get them released. After a month of pushing Karim and people within the federation, Maryam, her sister and her mother were finally released. However, I wasn't able to see her because as soon as she and her family were out of prison, they fled the country with the help of the Australian government. I never got to say goodbye to Maryam, and none of my attempts to contact her ever received a reply. Wherever she was, I hoped she had found joy again. Yet again, I had made a strong connection and it had been taken away from me.

Even then, I refused to back down. In fact, what had happened to Maryam made me even more determined. If they could find a way to destroy someone as strong as Maryam, then what about all those other girls who weren't as strong as her? We needed to be even stronger for them. We started extending the reach of our camps and festivals and expanding on what they did. It was no longer just football. The presence of NGOs and their financing meant we could run workshops with girls on forced marriages, on child marriages, on communicating with parents.

I was working all hours of the day and studying at night. I needed to make the most of the opportunities afforded me because I knew they wouldn't last forever. I wanted to kick open as many doors as possible before I was kicked out of one. I felt crippled with loneliness despite my ever-expanding football family inside and outside the country, because there was no one I could share my vulnerabilities with.

I was trying to maintain my image as a role model while still trying to learn. There were evenings when I would get home and slump into my room, overwhelmed and exhausted to the point of breaking. I couldn't talk to my teammates, because I didn't want them to know what I was going through. I didn't want to scare them or put them off. And I couldn't speak to my family because I didn't want their protectiveness to stop me from what I felt like I needed to achieve. I didn't want to add more barriers in my path. So, I would get home, sneak off to my room, sink my face into my pillow and had cry deeply. My oldest brother Shapoor had started working and had moved out, but Idris was there and could tell I was upset. He would come and sit with me in my room. I would fall asleep while the tears flowed. Then I would wake up, get back on my feet and begin again. Except I wasn't just on my feet, I was on my toes, at all times, trying to stay ahead in every game being played around me. I had to be on top of my game and think smart.

As always, playing football was a blessed escape, particularly during this time. The politics of the federation and the stress of Maryam being in prison were simplified when I played with the team. Here, I didn't have to worry about what people thought of me. All I had to do was stop the ball going into my opponent's net. So when the coach told me he had been put under pressure to drop me, I understood that this was their way of punishing me, by taking away my joy. Even though I said it was nothing, I had to swallow back the feeling of despair at the thought of not playing. I wished Maryam was there to talk to, to make a joke, to swear at them. I stood there, fighting back tears, on my own.

Well, I thought, if they were taking me off the pitch, I was going to have to work out other ways to win instead.

11

Football is a very simple game. But, like all simple things, it takes practice to do it well. To train until patterns become instinct, until you can't explain why or how you did what you did, how you knew your teammate would be there. You just did. Open your eyes.

My phone rang on the way to work, as my taxi weaved in and out of the Kabul morning traffic, the sound of car and motorbike horns blaring all around me. Oddly, it was a colleague from the federation office calling. Could whatever they wanted not wait until I arrived?

'Hello?'

'Khalida, the police are here. There was an explosion this morning. Karzai was supposed to be here for a ceremony. They're calling it an attempt on his life. They've arrested the workmen you hired and taken in some of the office staff for questioning. They're asking everyone about you. They have an arrest letter with your name on it. Your name is on all the documents. You have to stay away.'

Shit, shit, shit.

I asked the taxi driver to stop the car and let me out. I ran into a side alley, breathing hard. It was a sunny April morning and I was suddenly sweating. I felt like I couldn't breathe. I called Karim but there was no answer. I left voicemail after voicemail: 'What is going on? You told me to clear the office.'

His secretary said he was unavailable.

'You need to solve this,' I said agitatedly into the phone.

I wandered the backstreets, hiding in doorways. I tried to think back over the sequence of events that had led here. It had started with a football match called 'the Game of Friends'.

The previous autumn, 2010, with the help of Hummel I had arranged for our team to play a match against female Nato soldiers. It was the first time we had played a friendly in Afghanistan and I wanted to use it as a way of drawing attention to the team. I didn't really think the match would be a huge deal, but the idea seemed to gather momentum and, in the end, various media organisations from across the world turned up. I met Christian Stadil, the owner of Hummel, who flew over to meet the team to see what his sponsorship was achieving.

The game drew a crowd, a mostly male crowd of soldiers, translators and other staff working in and around the International Security Assistance Force (ISAF) compound. The soldiers didn't realise they were playing a group of Afghan women, and they were amazed and curious. They were very rarely in situations where they encountered any Afghan women. They only exited the compound to fight, before retreating to the relative safety of their enclosure, so this was new to them. They asked us questions about the team and about ourselves and we spoke to them.

My motivation had been to show these soldiers what they were fighting for, or rather, *who* they were fighting for. I desperately wanted to show them that there were many people in the country who wanted peace. I had seen the way they behaved around us when we went to our training pitch at the airbase, how suspicious they were. Their primary interaction with Afghans was with men, with fighters and fundamentalists. I thought it was important to show them that there was more to the population, that there was a human face to the country too.

This was important on both sides. All we ever saw in videos and photos was men, so seeing women soldiers was weird too.

We also didn't usually see the faces of soldiers. But there were women of different ages and backgrounds. Many of them had never met someone from Afghanistan who spoke English. They hadn't seen women at all.

'It's crazy,' Sarah, one of the soldiers, said to me after we'd kicked a ball back and forth for a while. 'I've not seen a woman's face the whole time I've been here.' She told me she was from a town in the middle of America, where it was always green. She wasn't used to the colours of Afghanistan, the soil and sand. She had played 'soccer' – as she called it – at college. When the game started, at first they seemed wary of playing too hard, as if we were fragile. But then the first hard tackle went in and that was it. We ran and we shouted. We laughed and applauded. At the end of the game, some of the players embraced. Sarah came and shook my hand.

'Well played,' she said before turning and walking back across the grass.

Whilst the exposure from the game was great PR for the team, it was also scary and dangerous. I was the organiser, the face for the federation, the team and the match. Consequently, I did interview after interview, and my face was everywhere.

'What if the Taliban shows up?' one reporter asked.

'I don't care. We will just continue playing football.'

Of course I cared and of course I was afraid for everyone's safety. But what people didn't seem to understand, what I had explained to my own father many times before, is that we were always in danger anyway, regardless of what we did. The threat of the Taliban was no reason to not do something, otherwise they would win.

When Karim found out about the match, he was furious. 'What the fuck have you done?' he raged. He had known there was going to be a friendly, but he hadn't paid much attention to the details and had no idea it would attract so much interest. 'This is so scary,' he said. 'It puts us in the most dangerous of places because we are letting women play against foreign soldiers. We will get attacked by the Taliban; you've put a target on the back of the federation. It's the most dangerous thing you have ever done.'

I had not done it intentionally.

'Listen, I didn't think about the Taliban,' I barked back, maybe a little too petulantly. 'I was thinking more about the world seeing the women of Afghanistan. It's a positive thing.'

What was more worrying was that it had *really* upset the new president of the NOC, a man called Zahir Aghbar, a former chief of the national police. He was in his mid-forties, intense and ambitious. I had caught his eye the previous year when I had started playing tennis at the federation court and hired one of the tennis coaches to train me in the morning before work. When he got wind of this, he began showing up. I always wore the loosest, least feminine clothes I could find as this made me feel safer. He would continue to offer to play against me. And he would come to the Football Federation's office to find me.

Some months before, Karim had become a governor of one of the Afghan provinces. He was becoming more powerful and spent less and less time in the building. So myself and two of my colleagues were essentially running the federation. Karim would check in with phone calls, but we were left to manage the running of the organisation. It became a second home, and the colleagues who I befriended there were a second family to me. In Afghanistan, our weekend is Thursdays and Fridays, and I would spend those days at work. I was there seven days a week, from early morning until late into the evenings. My identity felt increasingly intertwined with the federation.

There had always been a tension between the NOC and the Football Federation. Aghbar probably saw an opportunity to expand his empire with Karim away, or perhaps he was just curious about who this woman was, this woman who his rival supported. Once he found out how much Karim relied on me, his interest grew stronger.

His visits became more frequent. I heard he was asking all sorts of questions about me and my family. Aghbar would appear at many of the events I attended, his guards close by.

After a bomb was detonated at the Nato airfield one day, some time before the Game of Friends, no one from Afghanistan was allowed to enter the premises, which meant that we had to stop training. I petitioned the federation and the NOC again and again to let us train somewhere else, and finally they agreed. They didn't, however, give us access to the stadium. Instead, we were on the asphalt basketball court beside the stadium, or using the indoor facilities. It was slight progress, but it meant that we were even more exposed. There were more people around, and we were more visible. I was fiercely protective of the players. If anyone went near them, I would shout: 'Who you are? Why are you watching us? We are training. Leave, now! You are putting everyone in an uncomfortable position.'

The team was really flourishing and happy in the new environment. But Aghbar was noticing my activities and power with increasing interest. He continued to come to my office. When I went abroad, I bought fancy napkins from different cities and put them in my office when I returned. He would stand in the doorway and ask to take a napkin, snatching one up despite my refusal. He even asked to keep the special box they came in. Every rejection from me just appeared to make things worse.

When it came to organising the Game of Friends, we had an invitation hand-delivered to him. He opened it, read it, summoned me and threw it in my face. 'I'm the president of the National Olympic Committee. Why am I not aware of this? Nobody got permission from me and now I'm being invited to an event I did not authorise. What the fuck is going on?'

I had gone there to be respectful, as a way of making peace with him. He had, literally, thrown it back at me.

'I don't take a salary from you,' I said. 'I don't work for you. I'm not your employee; you have no right to do that to me,' I snapped. 'If you have any comments and complaints, you can go to my boss, and my boss is Karim. I've invited you to this event. If you don't want to come, fine.'

I picked the card up from the floor and left, his incredulity burning into the back of me as I walked out. He felt attacked by me. He wasn't used to losing. Wherever he went, people followed and fawned over him, but that wasn't the case with me. I wasn't trying to be disrespectful; I was just being honest, being myself. I wasn't responding to him the way he wanted me to.

He tried everything to win me over: he started inviting me to his office and he phoned me relentlessly, questioning my every move and decision. I would send his minions back to him with the message that he had no right to call me and that I didn't work for him.

Sometimes, he would show up at our training sessions. He knew exactly what time we trained and would come directly into the gymnasium, loudly, slamming the door wide, bodyguards in tow. We didn't wear scarves at practice, because there were no men around, or at least there weren't supposed to be. He started attacking us for the lack of scarves. He would yell: 'Who is promoting this non-Islamic culture? You're Muslim women, you have to wear a hijab.' It was relentless, and I bore the brunt. The lack of scarves was my fault, as head of the women's football committee, and he would stare me down. He called me disorganised and uneducated in front of my teammates, accusing me of being irresponsible and rogue.

My teammates were baffled. 'What have you done to this guy to make him so rude to you?' said Jamila, the left back with the thunderous left foot, who had become a real leader in the team. 'Can't you just call Karim and ask him to help? Why is he giving you such a hard time?'

But I knew that sharing what was happening with others would make them a target too. I felt as if the safest thing for everyone else was for me to take the full weight of the situation on my shoulders. On one level, I knew that refusing the support of my sisters was stupid, but I also wanted to protect them from the watchful eye of Aghbar. At exactly the moment I needed them most, I found myself pulling back from them.

In one training session I was so overwhelmed by the constant stress that I passed out. I was dribbling the ball slowly along and suddenly I couldn't see anything; it was like a dark curtain had fallen across my eyes. I felt dizzy, off balance. I couldn't breathe; I was gasping for air, silently. I was exhausted, mentally and physically. At the same time, I was trying my best to hide what was happening from everyone. I forced my eyes open, kept my head down and stumbled outside to suck in some fresh air and find some rhythm to my breathing. It was a panic attack. I felt like someone had grabbed my throat and squeezed it tight. My chest was burning. It felt like it was ripping apart. As soon as I could, I left the training session.

After that I stopped going back. The one place that had given me a kind of peace and freedom, the one place where I felt alive and happy, didn't feel the same any more. Aghbar was taking it away slowly, every time he showed up. I no longer felt safe there.

When the team showed up to train one day, they were turned away by one of his bodyguards and denied access. The team blamed me, saying that my actions had cost them their pitch and their opportunity to play. That was the toughest and most brutal of attacks, my teammates turning against me. They all came to my office and looked at me and said: 'Look, we had one thing that made us feel happy and empowered. This one hour of training has been taken away from us. Does this mean that we will not be able to continue playing?'

That was extremely painful for me. My fight was to create opportunities for women and now my fight was taking them away. This was not new. The NOC and the Football Federation regularly attempted to pit us against each other to break the team apart. They would work to build influence within their team, targeting the players who were easiest to manipulate, through either promises or threats. Efforts were made to tarnish my reputation, to imply that the team's interests weren't my priority. I was labelled selfish, a bad leader, aggressive, power-hungry and ego-driven. They plotted to poison the team against me while painting themselves as the saviours of the team.

Someone phoned schools where I had organised tournaments, and the national team players who were sent there to coach were turned away on arrival: 'Sorry, we are not actually allowed to let you come into the school and deliver this programme, because we were told not to.'

Then, ahead of a 2010 training camp to prepare for the South Asian Games, Aghbar blocked my service passport to prevent me from travelling with the team. Not many women in Afghanistan have service passports. Ours were provided by the government to allow us to travel to play football internationally, but the process was tightly controlled. When the passports were sent to the foreign ministry for visas, mine was held back. I had already anticipated that this was going to happen, so I was two steps ahead. I already had a standard citizen passport and I applied for a visa with that.

Things went from bad to worse. I had received threatening messages ever since my appointment in the federation was announced, but now both my family and I began to receive phone calls and messages. Constantly, every day. It never stopped. They threatened me and my family. They threatened to kill me. They said that I would be raped and they would take photos of my naked body and put them up everywhere. The story that our society was becoming more modern – that it was adopting women's rights and had moved on from the views of the Taliban – was a lie. The same poison existed, below the surface, waiting to erupt. It was bubbling out, every day, in the threats I was receiving, which were always violent. And, more often than not, I was sexualised within their violent fantasies. It was terrifying.

I began to recognise the same faces around me in the street and realised I was being followed. They didn't do anything, but the threat was clear. They could get to me any time they wanted to. Then there were a series of incidents on the way to and from training. Even though I had been dropped from the team, I still attended training, partly to show them they hadn't won, but also to show my fellow players I wasn't intimidated by anything they did to me. But now the same group of men would crowd around me, block my path, threaten me and attempt to intimidate me.

Those actively opposing me were taking ownership of my life, restricting my ability to operate freely within my city. I couldn't go anywhere without the constant threat or presence around me. I couldn't go to a restaurant or the shops. I had to have a driver, who would deliver me to and from work safely. I was so worried that my family would be targeted, in particular my brothers. It would be worse than bloody noses if they fought with these men.

Karim worked hard to protect me during this time, and I was grateful. It was one way he won my trust further. He organised the driver and car that safely chaperoned me everywhere. He never asked anything inappropriate of me. Instead, he supported me, and I naively assumed his motives were as simple as a desire to see me kept safe from harm.

I had filtered into all areas of the federation's work, including men's and grassroots football, and I was often left in charge when Karim was absent. My colleagues went along with me being in that position, but they didn't like it and I was aware of that. I felt increasingly wary of them. I became paranoid. I didn't trust anyone. I knew that the people I was working with were not my friends – very far from it. In addition to the threats I was receiving, my coach had started to receive threats on his life. I was scared – for the coach, for myself and for my family. I couldn't look left or right without hesitation and suspicion; it was everywhere, and it was relentless. I started changing my number regularly, ditching burner sim cards as frequently as any drug dealer to try and avoid the constant messages.

One afternoon, I was travelling in the safety car when I noticed a car behind us. I watched. Something inside me told me it was following us. Then, I saw the car accelerate, but it all happened so fast that I couldn't really register what was happening. The force of the impact took my breath away. The sound was like a gunshot. My head was ringing. I was thrown forward by the force of the car slamming into us. I tried to focus. I touched my lip, which I had caught with my watch on impact, but it wasn't bleeding, just throbbing. I looked up at the driver, who looked dazed. Then I craned my neck round to look out of the back window. The vehicle that had driven hard into the back of us was close, and the hood was crumpled. A gunman was climbing out of one of the windows. The sight of his body emerging from the vehicle whipped me out of myself. I thought: this is the moment that I am going to die.

Hooking my arm through my backpack and pushing the car door open, I stumbled out. I couldn't stand properly, my balance was off, but I gathered myself anyway and ran. We were in the middle of Kabul, and the traffic was dense and heavy, which, thankfully, was to my advantage. I ducked and dived between the cars, with eyes following me, people staring, until I was far away enough to stop heads turning. I tried to keep out of sight of my pursuers. I didn't know where they were or who they were, but I waited until I thought I could vanish around a corner without being seen. I didn't know where I was going, but I knew I needed to just keep running. Eventually, I found a quiet place where I could stop. I waited for a while, until I knew it was safe to phone my dad to come and pick me up. When his car pulled up, I collapsed into it, lying across the back seat, breathing freely for the first time in hours.

Later that evening, I sat quietly beside my parents.

'Have you thought about us at any point?' my father asked. It was a bruising line from him, but I knew it came from worry. 'They can kill you. You're a pawn, you're being used. Have you thought anything about that?'

'I feel like I'm trapped in a game,' I said.

'You are being used and you are not under eighteen anymore. You are an adult, a grown woman. You could end up in prison, Khalida. I cannot do time for you now that you're an adult. They can do whatever they want to you in prison; you wouldn't be safe there. I wouldn't be able to help or save you.' He paused. 'Have you thought about us?'

I felt lost. So unbelievably lost. I had no answer. I sat in silence, under the burden of the questions that my father had every right to ask. Yet, stopping wasn't an option for me. I could not quit. I didn't know what to do, so I just kept going.

I received letter after letter of complaint from Aghbar and his lackeys, demanding I go to the NOC office to explain what authority I had to organise the Game of Friends. They declared that I'd put lives in danger by doing so and, as an extension, put the position of sport in danger. I ignored them. 'Fuck you,' was my only thought. I had tried to involve the NOC in the development of women's football but had been brushed aside, and now they were trying to undermine my work. No. I responded with the same answer, time and time again: 'Karim is my boss. Go and speak to him. I took the decision. I had the power, and I took the decision because he gave me the power to do so.'

When the team was blocked from the training ground, I called allies in the media together to speak out against what was happening. It was breaking news. I was interviewed live on the six o'clock evening news, where I was honest about my fears for my safety. 'I know they are coming after me,' I said. 'This is my last moment. I know things are becoming worse and more dangerous. I have had a feeling that I will get shot, kidnapped, or raped.'

I named those involved and what had been happening on air. I was the first woman, to my knowledge, to speak this way so publicly. Yet, such is the culture of Afghanistan that I was blamed: 'Why didn't you leave? Why didn't you give up? Why are you fighting?' This was viewed as my fault. Even my own grandmother, my maternal grandmother, asked me why I was doing what I was doing. I was dismissive, and I said I didn't care. I was good at behaving cold and uncaring, but inside I hurt.

I knew there would be a cost to what I was getting myself involved in. I knew that I had a very short time at the federation, and I did my best to maximise that. I had achieved a position of power, and I had brought other women into the federation. I had found money, and though most of it never went anywhere near women's football, we had continued to hold events across the country. There were girls playing football in numbers never before seen in the history of the country. A generation of girls were experiencing what it was like to be part of a team.

I had made sacrifices to show women a different way, a different perspective on the world. As soon as my time was up, it would be up to them if they wanted to continue my battles or not. I had laid the foundations and if I was to be killed, it was the price I was prepared to pay to do so. That was my mindset and so I was not scared – not for myself at least. But I was scared of what would happen to my family.

I was tipped over the edge on Warlord's Day, a big celebration of when the Russians were forced out of our country. For the festivities Aghbar rented the football stadium that we had not been allowed to play in. Armies of people marched across the pitch in front of Karzai, their boots stomping down heavily on the turf that we had been forbidden to walk on. We had been told that our presence would destroy the pitch, and now I was witnessing helicopters landing on it.

I was so angry, I called one of the main TV networks. I told them, 'Our women's national team has been prevented from playing in the stadium they are now leasing out for events.'

They came down and filmed the helicopters landing and soldiers marching. They interviewed me and the players, and I spoke up against Aghbar during multiple interviews. I accused him of taking my passport and of using me in his vendetta against Karim. I had decided to finally show the world what was going on.

But then, Shapoor was attacked at his university by an unknown man with a knife. His leather jacket was ripped apart and he was injured badly, but he survived. At the same time Aghbar and a representative from the defence ministry strode into my office, flanked by their bodyguards, some of whom were armed. I didn't have my scarf on; it was on the floor. The NOC president reached out and grabbed my hand and lifted me from my chair. Pain ripped through my hand and up my arm as he yanked me to my feet. I was trying to squirm away. 'You're complaining, you're bringing in the media. You know the consequences. Have you thought about the consequences?'

'Have you?' I said, pointing at Karim's camera pointing at us. 'Everything in this office gets recorded.'

He looked from the camera to my face and then, still holding my hand tightly, he said: 'You started this game. Let's just see what happens.' And he left my office, slamming the door behind him.

I sank into my chair, massaging my injured hand. But I didn't have much time to think, because within hours we received a letter telling us that the federation needed to leave the offices of the NOC immediately. We needed to empty our offices and leave the place. I called Karim and explained what had happened in my office and the threats made. He told me to leave and find somewhere to operate from temporarily, with another colleague, until the new building the federation was due to move into anyway was ready. He told me that as the finance officer I was authorised to take money, rent a place and strip the office bare: 'Get everything, do not leave anything behind. We have builders; hire carpenters and get everything taken down.'

So, I coordinated the clearing of the office, and I helped too. I pulled a chair across and climbed up onto it, standing next to the window, to take down a big poster of my hero, Ronaldinho. I slipped a knife behind the corners where the old Blu-tack had hardened, trying not to damage the edges. I loved Ronaldinho. I loved the Brazil team, the flair, the colours; it all contrasted so sharply with life in Afghanistan. I would dream of the explosion of samba in the face of the rigidity of life for women in my country.

As I tussled with the top left-hand corner of the poster, I caught sight of a man standing below, holding a video camera pointed up at me. I had no idea what was going on. I scrambled down from the chair and raced outside to ask him what he was doing, but I was too slow. By the time I was outside, he was racing away at speed. I shrugged and got on with the office clearance I had been ordered to coordinate. As I was taking posters down from the wall in the corridor with a kitchen knife, I noticed another person filming me. I called out, 'Hey!' and jumped down from the chair to confront them, but they ran away before I could get close. Once everything in the building was clear and I had paid the carpenters for their work tearing down the internal walls, I went home.

The following morning, as I was preparing to go into work as usual, I received the call from my colleague, explaining that the police were searching for me.

I spent the next hour hiding in backstreets, trying to make sure that no one had seen me. Then I called Amir.

Over the last year or so we had fallen in love. Or at least I thought it was love. It had started with him supposedly 'tutoring' me in how to be a pious woman so that I would not be failed by one of the other lecturers. But we had stayed in touch when I had left university. We would meet in cafes and restaurants where nobody knew us. It was risky, as I was so far from being the sort of woman his family would have accepted, and I knew how dangerous it would be if Karim found out about us. An unmarried woman seeing a man alone would be hugely damaging to the reputation of the federation, and crushing to my own reputation.

Amir worked for the government. We would try and see each other every day, sitting in a cafe off the beaten track, talking for hours about anything and everything. He would drop me home in a taxi and leave. Nobody knew and they could never know. Perhaps what made me love him so intensely was that I knew there was no way it could last. Perhaps it wasn't love at all, really; perhaps it was just finally having someone I could talk to, someone who I could trust.

I was under huge pressure from my mother and grandmother to get married and settle down. It was unusual for a woman to be alone into her twenties. They wanted me to be married not so much because they thought I should be, but because they thought a ring on my finger would help protect me. My mum was worried and felt that me being married would help protect my name and my reputation and reduce the harassment and abuse. In the federation building I was regularly approached and propositioned. They thought they could have affairs with me – why else was I there? I had to be a prostitute, serving the president and able to serve them too. It made me feel quite sorry for myself and I played my femininity down heavily in an attempt to not give out any wrong signals. The tone of my voice, the language I used, it all became quite masculine. I swore a lot just to make myself seem off-putting and unattractive.

But after one too many times when my mother and grandmother had invited a man around to the house, and I turned up hours late and spoke honestly about what I wanted for my future, they finally backed off a little. In contrast to my mum, and sharply bucking the traditional expectations that fathers have of daughters in Afghanistan, my father and grandfather hated the idea of me being married. Each time my mother and grandmother would talk about bringing someone home for me to meet, you could see the sadness in their faces.

'Let her be free. Let her have her freedom. She doesn't need a man,' my dad had always said. They didn't want me to leave them. The men and women of my family were like two opposing teams, with me the referee in the middle.

I spent so much of my life hiding my true feelings that my time with Amir felt like the only time I could truly be myself. One way we would steal time together would be to travel outside of the country. I went to India with him, to Dubai and Pakistan, where we were free to be with each other in public. He was always saying I should leave the Football Federation, that it was too dangerous for me to stay. But I knew that the minute I gave up on my passion for sport and women's rights I would regret it.

That morning, when I called him in a blind panic, he answered the phone immediately.

'Where the hell are you? I just saw the news.'

'I don't know what to do,' I breathed despairingly. I explained what had happened.

'OK, don't go to any place where they can find you. Go into the national garden, they will never think that you will go to a public place, in plain sight. They will assume that you will hide at home or with a friend or relative.' He sounded concerned. Scared. 'Go to a public place. Sit somewhere in the corner. Stay away from people. Just go sit under a tree. Let's figure this out and keep calling Karim.'

I could tell that he was angry with me too. 'Why didn't you get anything in writing? How can you prove that you haven't coordinated this explosion? This is a government area. This is a government office. Are you seriously telling me you have no documentation to prove that you were told to hire those builders and then leave?'

'I don't have any proof,' I said, ashamed and defeated. It was only when I was sitting with my back against a tree in the Women's Garden that I realised just how dangerous a situation I was in. I called Karim, and this time he answered. I felt a surge of relief, but only the smallest of swells. He urged me to come back to the city and I heeded his advice, not worrying about being arrested. I headed towards the office that I had steered clear of all day and found Karim waiting nearby, out of sight of the building itself.

'Why the fuck did you do this?' he barked.

'What?' I reeled. What did he mean? Surely he didn't think that I had actually bombed the building? Surely?

'You told me to pay the carpenters to take down the internal partitions.'

I had seen the state of the place: the building had been almost levelled. Colleagues had sent me photos of what was left.

'You fucked it up,' he hissed. 'They have video evidence that it was you. They have a video of you with a large knife hacking away at the wall. They have proof and we can't save you. Why did you do that? Why did you get yourself involved in that?'

The video. The man I had seen disappearing down the corridor. I felt my stomach sink deeply. It had been planned.

'You told us to leave the building,' I said.

'I told you to take your documents and leave,' he said calmly. 'I didn't tell you to take anything. When did I say that? Do you have proof?'

That was when I realised I had been set up. I understood that now. To both sides, I was a liability. I couldn't be tamed or silenced.

My head was swimming, searching for ideas of where to go next and what to do, while the clock ticked and my time was running out. I left Karim and headed to a house rented by the federation that was occasionally used for meetings while construction was going on at the federation's offices, but I didn't stay long. My hands were tied, as I had no proof of my innocence. The news kept rolling and the workmen were interviewed, telling reporters that they had been told by a woman, a Khalida Popal, to destroy everything, and that she had paid them to do it. They claimed innocence; they had no idea. They were just workers, hired hands.

My phone was exploding. Back home my parents were inundated too. They were under attack from all angles, including our own family. My photo was everywhere, alongside those of two colleagues. We were being accused of planning an attack on the president and an investigation into whether we had planted bombs in the destroyed toilets was underway. The event the president had been set to attend had been moved prior to all this; he wasn't even there. The premeditation and set-up was clear to me. I was being hammered in the media for going against my country, for promoting non-religious culture, and they speculated that I was being brainwashed by the Western world.

I had been to the prison when I visited Maryam. I had seen women who were being held on much flimsier evidence than they had against me. Worse, we all knew of families where women had disappeared after being accused of bringing shame on their families. What if I were to just disappear? Many people had sent messages threatening me. It would be all too easy to blame a man who had gone too far, outraged by my dishonourable behaviour.

'Whatever you do, you need to leave as soon as possible. I can't save you,' my dad said to me in a hurried call. I couldn't let my brothers know what was happening, in case it put them at risk.

I tried to keep as low a profile as possible as I worked at masking my identity. I couldn't risk alerting people as I left the country. I reached out to contacts I had in various government institutions that could help get me a certified passport but with a fake name on it, one that wouldn't alert the authorities, and my family helped coordinate my transport to the airport. I hid around the Women's Garden and then later I was smuggled to more distant relatives, so I couldn't be tracked or found at home.

The night before I left, however, I went home. Everyone was asleep, as I stole in late at night. Nobody knew exactly when I was leaving, for their own safety. I myself wasn't even totally sure, until a few hours before my flight. All I took from the house was a backpack and a photo of the team, and I slipped out into the yard. It was early, and I stopped and just stood there for a moment, looking around our yard, overwhelmed by a sense of déjà vu. I wanted to remember more of it this time, so I stared hard, trying to sear the images of our house, the trees, the grass, the walls, into my memory permanently. I was startled when the door clicked behind me, and it wasn't my dad. It was my grandfather.

'Where are you going?' he said.

'I've got a meeting,' I stammered. 'I'm going on behalf of work.'

He saw right through me. He knew what was going on, he watched the news religiously.

'I think you're leaving and not coming back,' he said.

I was very close to tears, and I was doing everything I could to hold myself together. 'I'm not sure. I don't know anything right now. I can't answer whether I'm leaving or not. Please don't say anything. Don't tell anyone you've seen me.'

Tears spilled down his cheeks. He was older, frailer. I felt like a mother leaving her small child at the kindergarten gates.

I didn't want to hug my grandfather, and I didn't say goodbye – I couldn't. I had to leave right away; one more minute and I would never have stepped through the gate. I got into the taxi to the airport, disguised in different clothes to what I usually wore, and wearing a scarf fastened as neatly as I could manage.

Amir was at the airport. When I saw him my body began to shake; it felt as though I was being torn in two. I could barely put one foot in front of the other. I just looked at him. We couldn't speak, and we couldn't touch because of the risk that we were being watched. Just being connected to me would have put him in danger. So we just stood and looked at each other. Then, he walked away.

I only had a few minutes before my departure. That had been our plan: I would be the last person on the plane, so I wouldn't have to stand and wait anywhere or have to interact with people. I wasn't worried as I went through security. I had my fake passport and there were no biometrics at that time.

I boarded the plane and slumped into my seat. I cowered into it, trying to hide in plain sight.

I was devastated. I felt like I had lost. I'm a very competitive person and accepting any form of defeat has always been difficult for me. In fleeing I was giving up and letting them win. Their attempt to frame me, even if it hadn't resulted in my arrest, had succeeded in getting rid of me. They took everything from me. I was being forced to abandon my country and the people who I loved, and travel to a destination where I had no idea what was waiting for me. I was in shock. In denial too. I thought I would come back in a few months' time, and perhaps everything would be fine . . . people would forget. But the minute the wheels left the runway, I felt like my heart was crumbling into pieces, and I cried. I cried until the plane landed in Delhi. For the second time in my life, I was forced to leave my homeland.

12

Norway, 2011

Football is a low-scoring game. In most other team sports, more points are scored over the course of a match. But in football, most games are won by the odd goal. This means that the stakes of scoring or allowing a goal are larger. That split second before you celebrate a goal is a mixture of joy and something else: relief. Open your eyes.

'Hey!'

I was slumped on a bench at the side of the park next to the refugee centre, staring into space. I hadn't noticed the football that was rolling towards me. The girl gestured at it again. She waved at me.

'Hey! Hello?'

I pretended not to hear her and stayed sitting down. She shrugged and ran for it, turned with the ball and kicked it back to her friend. Somewhere inside, I registered that she was left-footed and not a bad striker. But it was as if I had a layer of concrete covering me.

The first months after I left Afghanistan were a whirl of activity. I spent my twenty-third birthday alone in Delhi, with absolutely no idea what I was going to do. I don't know what I would have done if hadn't been for Christian Stadil, the owner of Hummel, the Danish sports company. He was in touch constantly. We didn't really know each other, we had only met through work, but his staff embraced me like family. My savings and whatever I had been able to get from friends and family had been spent on the ticket to get me to the airport and out of the country in secret, so Hummel also supported me financially, assisting me with accommodation and food costs. Even the daughter of the CEO, Mette, was in touch, calling often just to talk. She told me it wasn't good for me to hold everything in, that it was important that I talk about what had happened to me. But I wasn't used to opening up and talking. I wasn't used to allowing myself to be vulnerable. And I wasn't coping very well. She had her own struggles, she worked full time, but she would check in regularly. She was compassionate and patient, a stranger's voice on the end of the phone, and eventually I began talking.

I was vulnerable, lost and alone, and she looked after me, as Hummel did. I couldn't burden my family. My former teammates had accused me of stealing money and skipping the country, poisoned by the lies of the federation, and I had no one to talk to. Mette didn't suggest solutions or make judgements. She just tried to understand and listen.

Anxiety attacks were frequent. On the rare occasions I did fall asleep, the nightmares would start. I would hallucinate a shadowy figure standing by the side of my bed as I thrashed around, trying to wake myself up, unsure of where I was. I had nightmares that I was back in the refugee camp in Pakistan. I begged the hotel for extra lamps so I could leave them on while I slept, so there would be no shadows. I was physically exhausted. My period lasted an entire month. Each morning I would wake up to my sheets soaked in blood. I was getting rashes all over my body. I wasn't eating properly. I wasn't myself.

The threats hadn't stopped either. I had the same phone number and there were death threats and messages coming through constantly. Only a small circle of people knew I had left the country. Two days after I had fled, a colleague sent me a scan of a letter addressed to me. It was a travel ban. I had managed to escape in the narrowest window. That woke me up to the scale of what was going on. I was used to things blowing over quickly. We all were: one day there would be an explosion, with hundreds of people dead, and a few days later life would return to normal. I thought that was the fate that awaited me – that I would disappear until things died down and then go back, but the travel ban exposed the naivety of that thought.

I called my dad and told him he needed to hide the family and keep a low profile. Especially my mum – she had to leave school and stop her involvement in sports, as she was too well known. My family were having to give up everything they knew as a result of what was happening to me. My mum had to say goodbye to the football team she coached. I had to tell her to sever all ties with the football community, because nobody could be trusted. They were at risk because they were tied to me. My brothers were shocked by me disappearing and didn't know what to say to me. Even Idris, who had always been able to talk to me about anything.

The clock was ticking. I needed to get out of India before my Indian visa expired. I had to move from hotel to hotel, hostel to hostel, constantly on the go as Hummel tried to find somewhere for me to stay. I tried to avoid places where there was any sort of large Afghan population. I stayed covered, and I felt nervous all the time. I didn't know what the outcome would be if I went to the Indian police: would I be protected or betrayed? One day, I caught sight of some people from the Indian Olympic Association, the equivalent of the NOC in Afghanistan, and I panicked, because I recognised the ones involved in football. I felt like I couldn't go anywhere.

At the same time, I was still trying to be there for my teammates. Especially for a young player called Gul, who was gay and had a complicated relationship with her gender identity. Her family had been so desperate for a son that they changed her name when she was a child and put her into a boys' school.

For the first seven or eight years of her life she was brought up believing she was the son of the family. She went to primary school as a boy and played football. Her identity was kept secret, even from her. Some years later, her mum gave birth to a boy and the family decided to change Gul's gender identity back to a girl. She was subsequently sent to a girls' school, where she had an identity crisis, unable to understand what had happened.

Before I fled Afghanistan, I had been supporting her through the trauma and confusion, acting as a mentor and a friend as best I could, but when I left, she crumbled. She sent me messages full of despair and anger and called me in floods of tears, unable to speak or breathe. I tried my best to support her, but I was struggling myself with my own problems, and I had to concentrate first and foremost on staying alive.

I had remained friends with a member of the team back in Afghanistan named Palwasha, who had replaced me as a defender. She was a woman of few words. She did her talking on the pitch, and you only had to watch her for a few minutes to know that she was strong. She reminded me a little of myself, though she was far more serious than me. I helped her and encouraged her to lead the team, because I didn't want the men to take over women's football. I worked hard in exile to get the team to Norway for the 2011 Norwegian Cup, one of the biggest youth tournaments in the world.

I was pretending to the team that I was travelling for work and that things were normal, but I was sure they knew exactly what was going on. It was all over the news. They read the papers. Still, they believed I would work something out, because I always found a way. The Football Federation, on the other hand, didn't notice or didn't care that I was helping; they were only interested in whether someone was doing work they could still take credit for. Trying to keep in contact with the team was partly selfish on my part too. It gave me something to concentrate on, something familiar to anchor myself to in a strange city where everything about my life was full of uncertainty. My family had gone off radar to protect themselves and I didn't want to put them in danger by contacting them. So, I kept in touch with the team through Palwasha and that sometimes helped me in moments when I felt unbearably alone.

The senior figures at Hummel were my only hope, and they knew it too. Eventually, after three months, they managed to get me to Denmark. I had to go to the Danish Embassy in New Delhi with my real passport this time, though I gave them the fake one too, because that was where my Indian visa was. I explained why I had two passports and they ran a background check which showed them exactly who I was. But I wasn't given a humanitarian visa. I was given a tourist one, and I flew to Aarhus to meet Stadil and his daughter. They took me to Hummel's office, where they kitted me out with clothes far better than the very small stash I had in my backpack.

The next day I turned up at the office and told them I wanted to work for them on their Afghanistan sponsorship.

'But why?' asked one of the Hummel team. 'Why would you want to help the men who have driven you from your home?'

'I'm not doing it for them,' I said. 'I'm doing it for the team.'

I knew that the team would not be punished as a substitute for me while I was in exile. The federation didn't need to punish them – they just needed to let everything we had built quietly wither, without helping it to survive or grow. I was determined not to let that happen.

I made the short trip from Denmark to Norway to meet the team, and when I walked into the meeting room to see them, we all burst into tears. Even Palwasha, who was so strong, came and held me, shaking. My suspicions were confirmed – they had all seen the news – but they embraced me regardless and called me their sister. For the first time in so long, I felt like I belonged. They wanted to know what would happen to us all now.

I caught up with my teammates and quickly realised that a number of the players were at risk.

First, I spoke to Gul in private. She was pale and thin. When she spoke, her voice was quiet. She twitched and she revealed that she had tried to take her own life twice in the time I had been away. I held her hands. 'We will make a plan,' I said. 'We will find a way.'

I could tell that if she went back to Afghanistan she would not survive. By this point there were some team members who I didn't really know very well, but there were three who remained from our trip to Pakistan. Taara, a hard-working forward; Veeda, who had been my partner in central defence; and Yasmoon, the ultimate substitute, who would play wherever she was needed. Separately, they all told me the same story. They had been taken aside by their families and told that this was their last trip: they would no longer be allowed to play football when they returned home, because they were to be married soon and it was time to grow up. They didn't tell me this as a drama. They just spoke sadly, resigned to it. It was a fact, like the diagnosis of an illness. As they told me their fates I saw a familiar look in their eyes. It made me think of Dahmina and I felt a lump in my throat. It was equal parts sadness and anger. How many times would our teammates have to feel those feelings? How many bodies would pile up as they forced us to stop playing? I just couldn't watch that happen again.

So at the end of the tournament, I helped Gul, along with Taara, Veeda and Yasmoon, to escape. I spoke to them all separately, quietly. I knew they trusted me and I knew they would be discreet, but still I had to know they wouldn't give the game away. I didn't know if there was any risk attached for me, I didn't know if I was breaking any rules, I didn't know if me helping these women would impact my family. All I knew is I wanted to save these women, or help them save themselves.

We smuggled Gul and the others away from the team, using people I trusted, and then we travelled to Sweden to seek asylum there.

When the rest of the team found out that we were gone, they were fiercely upset, and angry too. Not only had I left, but I had taken some of their teammates too. Some couldn't understand why I hadn't helped them. Some were still supportive of Karim, and they told him I had helped four girls escape. He called me, yelling down the phone, insulting me, threatening my family. He said he would put my parents in a private jail unless I returned to Afghanistan with these women in tow.

'I know how to get you back to Afghanistan and I know how to get you to get all those girls back to Afghanistan,' he said, calmly. 'Whatever you've done, I know where your mum and dad are. You will get these women back to Afghanistan and stop playing with the name and honour of the country.'

I couldn't explain to the team why those players needed to leave, for their safety, so I had to just take it all. The fury, the threats, the questions. The team stopped talking to me, and when I rejoined them I was frozen out of training and team meetings for the remainder of their trip. That nearly broke me. To have finally had a temporary feeling of belonging, during a time when I felt so vulnerable and alone in exile, only to have it snatched away from me again. It was unbearable.

I went to wave them off at the airport when they flew home, but the warmth and family sentiment that had been there when they had arrived was gone. Most of them didn't speak to me. Some even refused to look at me. I knew they thought I was selfish for staying in Europe. They couldn't understand why I had helped some of their teammates but not them. In seeing this on their faces and in their body language, I felt the overwhelming urge to return home, whatever the consequences. I felt homesickness like a physical ache at the centre of me. But

I also knew that helping those women escape had made it too dangerous for me to return.

I called my father in floods of tears.

'Wherever you are, you need to find a way to save yourself because Karim is really, really mad,' I said. My mum and dad were on speakerphone, but they weren't talking. 'He has threatened to come after you, to imprison you all. He knows that the only way to get at me is through you. Please, go and find a safe place to hide.'

I omitted any information about the missing girls and why Karim was suddenly so angry.

'Once again, you have chosen your teammates over the family,' said my dad, finally. 'Once again, you have chosen your mission and purpose over the family. And once again, you have put us in this position. You have put us all in danger, Khalida.'

I really didn't know what to say. He was right. I had been justifying my actions by pointing towards the team, and now the team didn't want anything to do with me. I had put my family in danger. I had jeopardised everything because I had to change things. But I felt like I had achieved nothing, because all it meant was that I couldn't go home. I imagined Karim sitting back in his chair smiling. I felt foolish and alone.

I kept supporting the players I had helped escape, with the asylum process and whatever else they needed. I neglected my future to focus on theirs, but it gave me a sense of purpose. I found that helping someone stopped me from focusing on what I had lost.

Once they were somewhat settled, I went to Norway to try and gain asylum there. My uncle – my mum's brother, who was closer to me in age than her – lived in Norway. He was my only relative in Scandinavia, so it made sense to go there. I didn't know what the asylum process was going to be like. First,

I went into the police station that handled asylum claims and handed over my passport. I explained why I was seeking asylum, but the two police officers just looked at me with bemused expressions.

'What documents do you have?'

I handed over everything I had.

'You are the first asylum seeker with so much documentation. Usually, asylum seekers don't have anything,' one of them said to me. 'They don't usually provide documents. Sometimes we even have a difficult time identifying which country they've come from.'

I had a big bag of things with me, including some sports clothing from Hummel, my backpack and my laptop. I was told I'd have to wait while they processed me.

'Can I go and get some coffee and something to eat from somewhere?' I asked.

They laughed again.

'Why is that funny?'

'Asylum seekers that come here don't ask if they can go for a coffee and grab a takeaway. You can't take any of your things with you. Leave everything here and we will keep it for you. Tomorrow morning you will be taken to the asylum centre, but tonight you must stay here.'

'Can I at least take my computer with me?' I asked. 'And my phone?'

They found that funny too and said that I couldn't. I would have to wait until the morning to get my stuff back.

When I returned, the officers took me to a room where I would stay for the night, a sort of holding cell for refugees while they are being processed. It was small and cramped, linked to another one adjacent to it. There was nothing in there apart from a single toilet, nowhere to bathe or shower, nothing. All I could do was sit and wait until my transfer in the morning. I had had no idea I'd have to stay there and was taken aback.

I still didn't understand the process and nobody made any effort to explain it.

'Can I keep my laptop?'

The officers looked at each other, slightly bemused, slightly sympathetically. They ushered me out of the room and closed the door behind us.

'Look, my shift is over, I don't mind driving you to the refugee centre,' one of them said. I think he felt sorry for me and wanted to protect me from being locked away for the night.

I stood out as unusual, having had support prior to my arrival there. I was treated more humanely as a result, which is sad, because if anything those who would be locked behind that door, struggling to get comfortable on the bare floor, needed humanity more than I did. Though I had tried to bury them deep, those memories of my experiences as a child in the refugee camp were still there. You never truly forget that every part of your life can be taken away from you. You never fully escape that fear. I may have been saved from that cramped room, but many others were still there, in a cell, despite having committed no crime.

We drove out of the city and then turned off the highway to an area in the middle of nowhere. It was late by the time we arrived, but the centre was still alive with movement and noise. I had never seen so many people from so many different countries in one place.

I was taken to a shared room with around eight women. The bathroom in the corridor was shared between a number of rooms, and everything was used and worn. I slung my backpack onto a spare top bunk and pushed my holdall into a cupboard. There was no privacy. I felt like I hadn't stopped moving for months. All I wanted was stillness and quiet, to try and process what had happened to me. I felt sure that's what everyone in that building wanted. But it's the one thing we didn't have. All

I wanted was to be alone – to cry, to mourn what I had lost. Instead, I was curled on my bunk with springs pressing into my back, trying to blur out the sounds around me, my laptop beside my legs under the cover because I didn't trust the lock on the cupboard.

In the morning I was summoned to have my biometrics taken and I was issued an ID card which displayed my status as an asylum seeker. I was told I would be there for at least a month while my claim was processed.

We were locked inside a building in the middle of nowhere, with no access to the city or local civilisation. There was a huge mix of people in the centre and there were drugs, alcohol and prostitution. Police would visit regularly in search of smugglers or dealers and remove them. It was so different to life in Afghanistan.

My computer was my lifeline. I still tried to work, coordinating Hummel's sponsorship of the teams, making sure the kit orders went through and trying to direct where the sponsorship money should be spent. All eight teams in the new men's league were supported by Hummel and the brand also sponsored the league itself. I coordinated their finances and administrative support from the refugee centre. Hummel were aware of where I was and what I was going through, but our relationship evolved to become solely professional as they stepped back and let the authorities take over my welfare support. I joined online meetings from the corner of a communal room, sent emails, spoke to the players and monitored the ones who had taken on my previous responsibilities back at the federation, guiding them on how to deal with Karim and the rest of the challenges they were facing. But I became more and more isolated and tired.

Nobody sleeps in a refugee centre. People stay awake to avoid the nightmares. We were all seeking shelter from different things, but we had similar stories. Of fleeing late at night, of deportation, of being stuck in airports in limbo and without an identity, unable to move forwards and unable to move backwards. In that centre we were all in limbo, waiting for the screech of police tyres outside at any hour, day or night, and expecting to be pulled from our room without even the chance to say goodbye and to not be seen again. Each day we would wake up with faces gone and new ones in their place. There was no privacy. We slept four or eight to a room in bunks. The toilets didn't lock and the showers were open, with no doors.

Working was my only relief, my only outlet, and so it was the only thing I did. I didn't want to talk to anyone. I didn't want to see people. I struggled to muster up the will to talk with my family back home. I started cutting off relationships with people. Every now and then I would receive an email from Amir, but I couldn't talk about what life as a refugee really looked like. How could I describe my surroundings, where everything was scuffed and broken, including the people? An atmosphere of resignation pervaded everything. All the rooms were full of people whose sleep was haunted by nightmares, a thing they all shared, yet the one thing they wanted to forget. When Amir won a scholarship to do his master's in the UK, I desperately clung onto the idea that we might be reunited at some point, but that was an island of hope in a sea of despair.

Karim was still furious, but the sponsorship deal for the Premier League of Afghanistan, and perhaps my distance, softened him. He acted like he forgave me. He contacted me by phone while I was in the centre. 'I loved you so much and I respected you so much,' he said. 'I've always seen you as a leader. You have given me so much stress and I've given so much stress to you. I gave you the freedom to take the lead. I never doubted your leadership. There is no way that those four women just escaped from the training camp without your help. It couldn't have happened while you were in charge.'

'Whatever they have chosen, it was for them,' I said. 'For *their* lives. They deserve to choose what they want. Let them have a better life, leave them alone and do not go after their families. Or mine. Just let us live in peace. I have given so much to the federation and I still do, despite you having repeatedly given up on me, and betrayed me.'

Hummel's sponsorship was significant and included the donation of a team bus for the men's national team to travel in. Clothes and equipment were sent too. But the players saw very little of what was sent. The bus was never used by the team. I tried to stay in touch with what was going on, but it became harder and harder to do so from a distance. I could tell that the federation were content to let the team die out quietly, as they continued to take the money for as long as possible. 'Well, we tried,' they would be able to say eventually. 'But there just wasn't enough interest in the end. No interest from our sisters to keep the team going.'

Months slipped by and my energy continued to fade. I didn't feel like myself any more; the fire and the energy that had once made me so passionate was gone. Then, one day, as the days were getting darker and the end of the year approached, I was called into the office and told that my claim for asylum to Norway was being rejected because of the EU double convention. I would be sent back to Denmark to seek asylum there. I was sent to a centre for rejected claims.

It was there that the football rolled towards me. It awoke something within me I hadn't realised had gone dormant.

From that moment, I started to get involved in the life of the centre. There were many refugees from Iran, Iraq and Somalia and I begin teaching a number of them computer and internet skills. That became my entertainment, being a computer teacher. I offered to help many women there too, translating conversations with doctors or social workers, or anything else they needed help with. In these quiet, practical exchanges, I began to feel connected to others and to the world again. Like fine threads, the act of being relied on, of being able to help others, began to reattach me to my life. I spent a lot of time with an Iranian taekwondo fighter who was struggling with suicidal thoughts. I tried to help him find a way out of those dark moments, to create structure in his life that would give him a reason to get up in the mornings. We spoke about sport, about what it represented and why it mattered. Speaking to someone who understood that gave me a sense of validation, of understanding. It was the first time I had integrated into any of the centres I'd been in.

I even started to shout out advice when I saw a game of football break out. It reminded me of our games in Kabul and, before that, when I was a young teenager in Pakistan. I thought of the millions of displaced people around the world, kicking a ball to pass the time, calling out to each other. Then I thought of Gul and the others who I had helped to flee to Sweden. I thought of the tens of millions of women and girls around the world who would never know that feeling. Football is a universal language, but it is also one that so many are not allowed to speak. In those dark days, I became determined to never stop shouting.

Just when I was settling into the familiar rhythms of the refugee centre, just as I began to know people by name, I found myself being escorted away by two policemen one morning. They took me to the front of the check-in queue at the airport, as the holidaymakers and business travellers whispered, wondering what the brown girl had done. They even came with me into the toilet, wearily saying, 'This is our job,' when I protested.

And with that, I was Denmark's problem.

13

There are different sorts of captains in a football team. There are those who shout, who inspire with their words. Then there are those who inspire with their actions. They do not need to talk. Open your eyes.

'Khalida!'

My brother, Idris, greeted me on the other end of the line. His voice was loud and happy. 'I just heard from Mum and Dad! This is such wonderful news. Read me the letter!'

I was standing outside the immigration centre, the gulls wheeling overhead. Since I had received the envelope with the letter confirming that I was to be granted asylum, after more than a year since I had returned to Denmark, I had hardly let it out of my sight. I knew the sentences off by heart. There were few words, but they meant everything.

As I read them out, Idris interrupted me to ask questions. My parents and I had agreed that we should all meet in India as soon as we were able to, and he immediately started suggesting what we would do, where we would visit and what we would see. He had always been like this, since he was a little boy. He would plan every last detail. Idris had started lecturing at the University of Engineering. He was living his dream, working on construction projects across the country. I said goodbye to him and went to bed that night, my head buzzing with thoughts of the future.

The next day, my parents called to tell me Idris was dead. He had been out for dinner with an Iraqi friend, newly arrived in

Afghanistan, and the restaurant they were in had been attacked. The driver of the group that Idris was with had seen some gunmen approaching the restaurant, but it happened too quickly; the group was attacked and Idris was shot. Their driver was injured but managed to slip away, and he phoned my dad to let them know what had happened. My dad recounted how he had raced to the restaurant to fetch Idris's body.

I put the phone down, completely numb. All I could hear was the excitement in my brother's voice from our phone call the day before. I still thought of him as the little boy I'd grown up with.

I had finally been told I could stay in Denmark, but all I wanted to do was go home. I couldn't keep my thoughts from racing. Was this Karim's doing? Had they done it to get to me? To get me to come home? Then I would catch myself spiralling and think, don't be ridiculous, this kind of violence happens often. This was a horrible mistake, a tragedy that he had been caught up in.

I was making my preparations to move out of the permanent refugee camp I had spent the last few months in. It was in the far north, a desolate, windy place with a population of under one thousand people, mainly former fishermen. Over the last year, I had lived in a succession of buildings, watched four whole seasons pass in Denmark. I had felt like I was toughening up, learning to survive, building myself back up, but my brother's death shattered me into a million pieces all over again. I couldn't take the pain. I suffered anxiety attacks all the time, and they only increased in intensity and frequency.

A year ago, in January 2012, I had arrived in Denmark from Norway with a train ticket and an address. I had no idea where I was going and I hadn't even had the opportunity to change money into Danish kroner. I stood at the station, lightheaded and hungry. When I arrived the asylum centre, I walked up to the front desk and declared: 'I'm an asylum seeker. I've been deported from Norway and I'm seeking asylum in Denmark.'

I was put in a waiting room. I was there for hours and hours until someone knelt by me and took my fingerprints. I had left the asylum centre in Oslo at around 5 a.m., and it was 5 p.m. before I asked if I could have some water.

'Just wait. Someone will come, then you will get all those things. There is a process,' I was told.

I was so sick of the word 'process'. I couldn't eat or drink until I had been registered, even though I was on the cusp of fainting. After my fingerprints were taken I had to sit with a headset on and listen to an hour-long explanation of Denmark's asylum rules, but I couldn't focus on what was being said. Tears prickled at the corners of my eyes from tiredness. I thought of the little girl who had demanded meat, or who had gone up against the football authorities at home. That person felt like someone else. Someone that little girl would never have imagined me being. I had been ground down.

Once we were done I was given some food. I almost collapsed onto my bed, in another shared room, and I slept deeply. The next morning, I got my bearings. I didn't even have a locker, just a curtain across a shelf. There was also no electricity in the bathroom. On my second night I was sitting on the loo in the pitch dark when the door swung open – a man's face loomed over me, he seemed intoxicated. I screamed and shouted until enough people came running in and steered him away.

The nightmares of someone looming in the shadows were back. I avoided going to the canteen and tried to encounter as few people as possible. I had a big coat and a cap and I tried to hide my face beneath them. I had tears in my eyes continuously; it was uncontrollable. I wasn't eating or sleeping properly, so I was fainting a lot. Twice I hit my head on the floor and once on the bunk bed. I no longer had the motivation to leave the bedroom, or even to get out of the bed.

It was December and it felt like it was permanently dark and raining. I lost count of how many times I moved from one centre to another – they merged into one and I was so withdrawn by this point that I hardly noticed the difference. The same cramped rooms, the same bunk beds. The same rain against the same dark windows. I couldn't bear to contact anyone I knew. I was still in contact with the football team in Afghanistan, but often I couldn't summon up the energy to reply; if I did, it was a short 'Yes' or 'No'. I could tell that the team still felt betrayed by me helping Gul and the others escape in Norway, and I couldn't face that on top of everything else.

My father had told me that the family had decided it was no longer safe for my mother to be in Afghanistan, and they had begun making arrangements for her to be taken to Europe. He was brief and business-like with me. He didn't blame me – he would never say that. But how could he not? I blamed myself. None of this would have happened if it wasn't for me. If I hadn't poked the wasps' nest. I had consoled myself all along that it was worth the risk. That I might get stung, but it would be in service of changing things for the better. But it was my family who were being stung. They were suffering for my choices and I was suffused with guilt.

As a part of phase two of my asylum 'process', I was interviewed. I was told: 'If you liked Norway and you really want to leave Denmark, you're more than welcome to. You can leave any time.'

I looked at the woman interviewing me.

'Do you think I'm stupid?' I said. 'They deported me. They don't want me. Where do you think I can go? Where? Which country? Do I have a choice? Can I choose any country? I don't have a choice. These are all bullshit rules and now, after I have wasted months of my life in Norway in different refugee centres, experiencing all the horrors within them, I come here and you act like I have a choice? I have zero choice. I'm stuck here. Let's just go on and start the interview.'

I could tell I had made her angry, but I felt weary and the questioning was stupid. I told her what had happened to me in Afghanistan, but she didn't seem to understand how it was possible.

'The Taliban left over ten years ago,' she said. 'Surely things are better?'

The questions I were asked were always framed as if women had the same fundamental rights and protections all over the world. I kept having to explain that this wasn't the case. In Afghanistan, to be a woman was to be a second-class citizen. To be a woman who angered the state meant being in an orbit of immediate danger that simply didn't exist in Denmark.

Over three interviews, the longest of which was ten hours, I told my story over and over again. I felt like I was in court, trying to make a case for why I deserved to be in their country, why I deserved protection. It was like I was negotiating for my existence. I had no idea who the person was that I was speaking to, why they were in this job, what their politics were. I just knew that I needed them to like me, to be on my side. So I repeated everything, again and again. I retraumatised myself repeatedly to try and save myself.

I found out a more right-wing party had taken charge of the country, and that they were very anti-immigration. After a few months, I was moved to the permanent camp by the sea, while I continued through the 'process'. There were rumours that everyone was getting rejected. I didn't know any Afghans who had had their claims approved, so I expected the worst. I would sit by the window, watching the seabirds and feeling jealous of their freedom.

One day, I was in my room when there was a knock on the door. One of the members of staff put his head around the door, looking worried, and asked me in English: 'Are you from Afghanistan?'

I nodded.

'We need someone to translate, urgently.'

He led me down the corridor to a room, where a woman was lying on a bunk. There was blood and broken glass on the floor.

'What is the matter?' I asked.

She just looked at me. They had turned her application down. I translated for them. She had been separated from her children in a crowd at the border crossing, so she had tried to climb back over the barbed-wire fence to go back and search for them. This meant returning to the country where her family wanted her dead for dishonour. She was unable to find her children. She had cried until she could no longer speak. Their names were the first thing she spoke in the morning and the last thing she said at night. She had tried to live for them, but it hurt too much to be without them. In this place, as we waited, like packages that had been sent to the wrong address, she couldn't do it any more. She needed it all to end.

As I told her story, as I held her hand, I came to see that though I had been through a lot, there were others who had been through more. Those who could not advocate for themselves. For the first time, I felt the flicker of the old me. The sound of my grandparents telling me to fight for what I believed in. I went back to visit that woman, her wrists swathed in bandages. I tried to help her see that the only thing she could do, to honour her children, was to live a full life. Not to do their work for them. To give herself the chance of returning and finding them.

I began translating and teaching at the centre, just as I had in Norway. And just like when I had visited Maryam in the prison in Afghanistan, I realised how lucky I was. At least the men who threatened me were not my family. Again and again, I heard stories of relatives turned on each other. To prove their own piety, to keep themselves safe. Families who had the Taliban inside them, who saw the world through their eyes. Girls who were rumoured to have had boyfriends and who knew that would be enough to get them killed. Mothers who tried to stop their daughters from being married off to older men. I had been fighting for the right to play football. But again and again I heard the stories of women who couldn't even dream of that.

I helped refugees connect with their families digitally. I taught them how to write letters or how to ride a bike – small practical things that reminded us all that we were human beings.

I started a female running club. We would go out just after the sun had gone down, so we would feel less visible and safe from the gazes of men. Most of us barely shared a common language, but it didn't matter. We recognised something in each other and as we ran, our bodies communicated without language. We ran faster, taking it in turns to lead and set the pace. In the simplest of human activities we found something that we all clearly needed. We put one foot after the other, again and again. And gradually we got stronger, and faster. We ran further.

'Keep pushing!' I'd shout. 'Imagine with every step you're beating those who made you leave your home.'

In this club, we shared laughter and we shared goals. I realised that when I was around these women, I felt the familiar feeling of kinship and community that I used to feel when I was with my football team. These women, who had been taught by experience that they didn't matter, found that this one tiny thing was theirs: in the act of putting one foot after the other, of feeling themselves getting quicker and stronger over the days and weeks.

I even briefly started playing football again, in a local amateur league, though I had to stop when I incurred a knee injury and needed surgery. There was no formal physiotherapy, so I would try and walk around the centre to keep it moving. Once, this would have knocked me down, but I was able to keep going. I threw myself into everything around me and the people I had come to know at the centre. It began to feel like we were building our own little community where we could share our pain, discuss our hopes and our fears.

It was into this context that the letter came, declaring the success of my application for residency. I was the only refugee from Afghanistan that I knew of whose application had been approved. Of the group of women I spent time with in the asylum centre, who had been interviewed before and after me, I was the only one who wasn't rejected in the first round. These women were no less deserving or desperate than me. The difference was that my plight was public: the documents were there for all to see, and my name and face had been plastered all over the Afghan press and I was known throughout the government. I had proof, whereas so many who flee do not.

Medina's case was high profile in Afghanistan too, but her situation demonstrates the problems with the asylum system. She didn't know how to tell her story in the way needed to get her asylum request approved. She was fifteen years old when her family fled to Pakistan, and she was married off almost immediately as a way of protecting her. Except she wasn't safe. Medina was married to a very conservative man from a very rich family, who moved her back to Afghanistan while her family found asylum in Denmark. As each of her five daughters was born, her in-laws became increasingly violent and disrespectful towards her. Her sixth child was a boy, but when he was three months old her husband was kidnapped and then killed, his body found dismembered in a bag. She was young, with six children, and living with abusive in-laws. She was routinely locked in the house. Eventually she escaped, with the help of a neighbour, and her parents paid smugglers to get her to Denmark.

She was desperate: she had lost her six children, the youngest still a baby. She would sit in the corner quietly crying, crippled with depression. Her husband's death had made the news, as his family was important, but she didn't know how to communicate her case in the way the authorities wanted. She was broken. This was the case for so many of the women in the centre. They were often traumatised and couldn't navigate the process, a process that would traumatise them further, a process that is designed to keep vulnerable people out. Medina was rejected twice and was issued with a letter saying she had thirty days to leave Denmark. I tried to help her, going back and forth with officials and translating for her. Before her thirty days were up she was granted a humanitarian residential permit.

I read out the short, official sentences in the letter I had received to Idris, and the next day he was dead.

I was numb. What should have been a celebration was a mourning. I moved out of the refugee centre to Helsingor, another city even further north. I didn't want to talk to anybody; I became a hermit. Every time I had clawed my way out of a desperate situation to reach some semblance of happiness and community, it seemed like something else – something even worse – would happen.

The government provided money for food and housing in temporary accommodation, a bit like a homeless shelter. My room constantly smelt of alcohol. It was crawling with bugs and there was birdshit everywhere just outside the building. Every day I would walk to the harbour and think about slipping into the dark water. I would stand and stare into it, my inner voice whispering to me: 'Go into the water, just finish this. Go into this water, you will feel comfort, you will sleep.' But my body didn't even have the energy to do that. I hadn't been sleeping, and my pain was so vivid it was physical. I didn't know that I had depression. I didn't know I needed help urgently. I had no idea that help existed, no awareness of what depression was or that it was treatable.

My family had lost all contact with my mother after they had managed to get her smuggled into Denmark. We didn't know where she was, or if she was still alive. So much pain had been caused by my actions. It was the lowest I had ever felt. Everywhere I looked was darkness.

Down at the harbour one day, I was sitting on a wall, looking into the water with tears in my eyes. I didn't notice that someone was watching me. It's very unusual for someone to approach a stranger and start up a conversation in Denmark – it's not the culture of the place – but the man who was watching me approached and started talking to me.

'Hey, where are you from?' he said. 'Do you speak Danish? Do you speak English? How are you? I've seen you here for the past few days. You look sad. Can I help?'

My first instinct was to not trust him, but he spoke gently to me and told me about himself. He was a train driver named Henrik. I don't know how, but he had sensed that I was drifting away from life, and he sat there next to me, talking to me. And, gradually, I drifted back a tiny bit. The next day I saw him again, and we talked again. Over the next few days, he began to help me fill in the paperwork I needed to start a new life in Denmark. I wanted to take Danish lessons and continue my education and get a job. This random act of kindness – speaking to a stranger who is at the lowest point in their life – meant everything to me. It made me feel like I could keep going.

I lived in temporary accommodation for three or four months. All the while I wanted to restart my education so I could get back to working properly. Except my existing qualifications weren't deemed good enough. I sat opposite a woman who was supposed to help me integrate, a bit like a social worker. She told me: 'Qualifications from Afghanistan are not accepted, as they aren't of the right standard. I think you should lower your ambitions, be realistic, and go back into year seven or maybe year eight.'

'But I've graduated from university with two degrees,' I said. 'I have a degree in teacher training and one in business management, and you're suggesting I go back into the first year of high school? I want to do a master's.'

The money I received from the government to aid my settlement just about covered my rent and bills. I had signed up to a three-year course at a language school, but I was determined to not spend the time it took to obtain a degree learning Danish.

I requested permission to change to a different language school where I could do an intensive six-month course, but I couldn't afford to travel there and back. So I asked whether I could get help with travel costs.

'You know what,' my contact for support said. 'You don't need to eat luxury food; you don't need to buy meat. Think about buying cheaper food so you can afford your ticket.'

In so many ways, as an asylum seeker, you are told you should be grateful just for being there. I decided that I wouldn't be. I would try to make my life better. I wrote letters and I learnt things as I went along. I asked for help from anyone who offered it. I found that demanding voice of the little girl inside me again, that girl who wasn't afraid to speak up and tell people what she wanted. After all, I reasoned, this wasn't Afghanistan, or men with guns; it was people giving me unfriendly looks. Within two months I had a job with the Danish Olympic Committee as a project manager for one of the charities they supported that ran football projects in the Balkans, and I had enrolled in the shorter language class.

My mother contacted me from an asylum centre, and though I knew the awful 'process' she would be going through, I was elated to know she was alive and in the same country as me.

It took several hours to get to the centre. The moment I saw her, I was struck by how thin and tired she looked. I broke down in tears. My gentle mother. Exiled from her beloved students. My mother, who would fall asleep reading every night and put the book under her pillow. Alone, in a strange country. Away from her husband and sons. Alone.

'I'm sorry,' I said. 'This is all my fault.'

She took my face in her hands. 'It is *their* fault,' she said.

She could see the depression that gripped me and her face was etched with concern for me. When it was time to leave my feet were leaden. I had to drag myself away, and I didn't want to leave her there. I stepped through my front door and shut it behind me, but I couldn't just accept the status quo. I turned and went straight back to bring her home with me. When I reached the centre it was late and I had to negotiate my way back in. My mother had fresh tear stains, mingled with old ones, down her cheeks and she looked scared. Getting her out wasn't as hard as I anticipated. I had to hand over my address and other contact details, but she was allowed to leave with me: one less person straining the system, one more bed ready to be filled.

When I got the job at the Danish Olympic Committee, I had stopped communicating with the social workers who had been appointed to work with me. But when I applied to do a marketing management degree at Copenhagen Business School and was accepted, I couldn't resist showing them that I had defied their expectations. I was working and studying and being told to slow down, except I knew where I wanted to be and there was no time to rest or have fun. There was no going out, no trying to socialise with people, find friends and build a community around myself. It was all work and study, work and study. I took education so seriously.

In Afghanistan, when you go to university, you make sure you are well prepared. On my first day at university in Denmark, I was the same. I was focused, serious, and I had my books ready. But it was a different world. The two tutors talked about the programme, but the two things that stood out was organising a date to go camping together and finishing at noon on Fridays so we could take advantage of the open bar and DJ. It was a culture shock. Particularly the drinking and the openness around it. I didn't drink – not for religious reasons, I just didn't want to. I didn't feel like I needed to. Coffee made me happy. There's a perception that when you don't drink it's also a barrier to you making friends and socialising with people. I learnt that in Danish culture people get drunk first, and then they socialise. In Afghanistan we don't drink, but we still go crazy. We don't need alcohol to make us sociable.

We are already very sociable. If anything, we need alcohol to calm us down.

I struggled academically because there was so much group work, and it became very socially based. The other students would bond over drinks without me, spend weekends together and organise groups around those friendships. I had to work around studying, travel to university and back, and fit in speaking engagements. Most of our grades were based on the delivery of projects that were being worked on in groups, but I never had a group. Where they could divide and conquer, with each student in a group of five delivering three pages, for example, I had to deliver fifteen myself. And it had to be good. I had earned my place there and I had to justify it.

I stopped working for the Danish Olympic Committee to work with asylum seekers as a social worker. I wanted to provide a better experience for those coming into the country than I'd had. I had ten newcomers to work with, young men and women. My task was to get them into education and work. They felt like family. Seeing them flourishing and growing in this new country filled me with joy. I had to travel two hours each way from university to be able to do it, which cut into the time I had to study, but I was like a machine rolling on day after day.

I had been shaken deeply by seeing my mother. One day, after I had sat frozen, unable to type and with tears silently rolling down my cheeks during a timed session in one of my classes, I realised I needed support with my mental health. My professor took me aside and asked me if I was OK. When I told him I was having trouble sleeping and eating, and felt constantly at the edge of darkness, he put me in touch with the mental health team at the university. They connected me with a local doctor.

I spent time in a centre that specialised in the sorts of trauma that migrants and refugees suffer from. There, for the first time, I began to truly understand what had happened to me. How much I had buried and never talked to anyone about. For the first time in a long time, it felt like someone had let light into the room. My professor had saved me. He had taken the initiative that so many people suffering with deep trauma and depression need. I was so overloaded by my trauma that picking up the phone for help, even calling a doctor, was not possible.

Henrik would drive me to and from my therapy sessions. He and others around me took charge of the small things that felt impossible, so I could focus on the big things that were all-consuming. Refugees lose everything and everyone, and they have no idea if they will ever see anyone they knew again. In the centres, you are free but you have no freedom – it's like a prison, even though it's not. You are stuck in the system and cannot reconnect with your life. Your identity, who you are and who you wanted to be, is dead. You may have been someone, had friends, studied, worked, but now you are starting again, a number on a card. Your education is not valid; your work experience is not to the right standard. If you're in your twenties you lose a decade or more of your life having to restart your education. It's like you're on rewind. I had to push hard against that, but few others have the support of people like Henrik, who translated from Danish for me, to do that. There are people in their thirties and forties who have to go back to university and start again. It is dehumanising and a waste of talent.

On weekends I supplemented my income by working in a cafe so I could practise my Danish, and that's how I managed to pass all my Danish tests. Though I had realised that I would never again be able to play because of my knee injury, I was starting to integrate into the footballing community of Denmark, running workshops and organising tournaments. I started to get some of the refugee women to go along to tournaments too. Time and time again, I saw the power of football, as these women, who had been forced to shut down so much of themselves to survive, responded to the game.

14

There are some sports you need lots of equipment for, or specialised space. But football is like a plant that grows up through the cracks in concrete. It flowers everywhere in the world. All you need is a ball. Open your eyes.

'OK, let me fix it. Where is the injury? Here?'

I stood quietly watching as the man moved his hand up the half-naked player's leg. 'Here?'

I had left the hotel room to go and get the first-aid kit. I had been gone for less than five minutes and in that time one of the male 'coaches' from Afghanistan had entered the room. He was sitting on the edge of the bed, murmuring to her.

'Hey, thank you,' she said. 'No, it's fine. I can take care of it, it's fine.'

She was scared. I could see it in her face and hear the panic in her voice.

'No, it's not here. It's under my knee.'

He was ignoring her, reaching up way past her knee, running his fingers to the top of her thigh. She was frozen, but then she snapped out of her trance and tried to pull the cover across herself and push him away. But she was small and injured and not sure what to do. She was uncomfortable, but she didn't know how to say no. She couldn't do anything. I stood there, shaking and furious.

I was with the team in Jordan for one of a series of training camps ahead of attempting to qualify for the 2019 World Cup. The path there had been a winding one.

★

It had begun the previous year, when I started to get phone calls from members of the team in Afghanistan. I was beginning to feel more connected to my life in Denmark, but they told me that they had returned from a training camp to news that the Football Federation planned to shut down the entire women's football committee, essentially giving up on women's football entirely. There were two reasons. The first was that the team was performing poorly and the second was that coaches were increasingly abusing or harassing players. The players also raised the issue with a number of organisations that had funded some of the team's programmes, such as the German FA and US Embassy. Then I started getting emails from the media about it.

I rang Karim and said: 'Foreigners, especially the embassies, have contacted me and asked about the situation with the women's committee. I haven't replied to them, but just remember one thing: we have worked really hard to bring women's football to where it is now. Regardless of their performance, regardless of what level they are at, it is so important to keep going, because the foundation has been built. The reason we play football is to promote women's rights. Shutting down the programme will hit you big time. It will be a breaking news story in the Western world, which means you will lose a lot. You will lose Hummel, the sponsor I brought in. They have been supporting the men's league as well and you will lose that. It's your decision. I'm not against it, but these are the consequences. Now, you choose if you want to continue or not.'

In addition, I offered to help rebuild the team and committee and put a strong strategy in place.

He called me again a couple of days later: 'OK, let's make this happen. You create your team. You have all the support from me, you have all the freedom. You just tell me how we should do it. Don't ask for money, just do it.'

I knew that I was only going to have one shot at this, and I wanted the Afghan women's team to experience what a professional environment was like. The first thing we needed were professional coaches. I sent emails out to people I'd met on the various courses, including the former US international coach, Kelly Lindsey. Some players had met her on a coaching course and she had offered to help support the team in any way she could. I tried to find out a bit about Kelly, but I struggled. She had no social media presence and there was barely any media on her. I sent her a long email, explaining who I was and what I wanted to achieve. My request was clear, black and white: there was no money; I needed a volunteer, a coach who would be willing to help me, first to re-establish the team and participate in the South Asian Games, and secondly to embark on a mission to get the team competing for a place at the 2019 World Cup.

At that time, Kelly was working in Hong Kong, but we managed to have a conversation. The moment I heard her voice I knew she was going to be the head coach. Then I found Haley Carter, a former goalkeeper, and she became Kelly's assistant. She was a former US Marine as well as a professional player. She was fun, full of fire and energy, extroverted and very organised. The three of us made a great team. We had regular video calls and we planned how we would work together. Those early planning meetings I had had with Samira, back when we pretended we were doing homework, seemed like a different world now.

I took everything I had learnt from my years in exile, about strength and sisterhood, about the need to feel an active part of a community, and I poured it into the team. We decided to set up a new framework: from inside Afghanistan, the best players from the league would be selected for the national team; from outside Afghanistan, women who were refugees but still involved in football and wanting to give back to Afghanistan could also try out for the team at any of the various training camps they could get to. We would apply for funding to cover their travel. The women in Afghanistan couldn't fully fight the system, but their sisters on the outside could, and they could elevate the aspirations of those in the country too and show them what life could hold for them. We had one chance and we had to take it.

Gradually, Kelly and Haley transformed the team. Kelly was such a natural leader, so humble and selfless. Though they were both based in the US, they sent huge numbers of training videos for the team to work through. And when we held the training camps abroad, Kelly made every player feel that she was at the heart of the team. She worked hard on breaking the ice and engaging both the new young players from Afghanistan, who we didn't know so well, and those who were playing abroad. The younger players didn't have the same trust or knowledge of me. They only knew me from what they had seen or heard in the media, and that was overwhelmingly negative, in Afghanistan at least. Gradually, though, they opened up and we began to see a team forming.

We had held trial camps in the Netherlands and invited the best players to a training camp in California. I had always felt so different to the women around me in Afghanistan. It was a male-dominated culture, and I found myself rallying against that from day one, but sometimes I felt alone because of it. In Kelly and Haley, I came to see similar characteristics. I related to them and I felt a newfound joy in that. They were women like me; it was wonderfully refreshing. And they believed in the project and would do anything to make it happen.

Kelly was fundraising, making use of her contacts in Hong Kong and elsewhere. We were bringing players together from all over the world and it was expensive. In between camps, Kelly would send players training videos to watch and things to work on virtually. Haley fundraised too. We were running a federation inside a federation – or, rather, outside it. We wrote letters to players' families to appeal for their release to travel;

the letters were sent to the federation to sign and stamp before going out.

But it wasn't without problems. The Football Federation were suspicious of foreigners, especially women. We might have had a good team on the pitch, but then players' names started to change on the lists sent to us by the federation. Some of the players we had called up weren't included. It was a familiar scenario. The excuses were that they had stopped playing football and didn't want to do it, that they had left the programme, but we knew these women. Their love for the game wouldn't have died so quickly and easily.

After the first camp, we were told we were all fired because one of the players, a seventeen-year-old, had curiously stepped into a strip club near the cheap hotel we were staying in. She had taken a picture and posted it on social media, and someone at the federation saw it. Karim called us up, ranting and raving, saying we had disgraced ever single player on the tour. I couldn't believe the girl had been so stupid, and we were very worried for the players travelling back to the country. Our top priority was protecting the players who had come directly from Afghanistan, since they would be the ones in immediate danger when they went home.

None of us were actually employed, so there was nothing really to fire us from, but shutting down the programme would impact the girls in Afghanistan. When I had started talking to Kelly, we said that we wanted to help players become coaches too. We wanted to train the next generation of the team's leadership – players who could take on our roles and lead and run the team. The hope was that we would train them, exit and then one day watch them playing on the biggest of stages, satisfied that the vision had come to fruition. I didn't want to fight on forever.

The pattern repeated with every training camp. Every time there would be some sort of incident that caused the federation to 'fire' us, but we would keep on doing the work. And eventually they would decide that the chance to take credit for our work was too tempting.

When we arrived at one of the training camps in 2017, there were two male 'coaches' who I'd never seen before. I assumed they were there as Karim's spies. But we had to focus, as one of the most important steps in the history of the team was about to happen. We were going to play a friendly game, which would get us an official FIFA ranking.

That's why, that first night at the training camp in Jordan, I decided I had seen enough.

I stepped into the room, and the coach leapt to his feet. I grabbed him and pushed him out of the room and threatened him. 'I'm going to report you!' I shouted as I pursued him. 'What you've done is not right. You'll never go back onto a pitch or into a classroom. You're not allowed. Stay away from here. I kicked you out of the room, I will get you kicked out of this country.'

His face was red and he was breathing heavily as he stood there, but I saw fear in his eyes too.

'What are you talking about? You're a crazy bitch. I don't know what you think you saw. No one will believe you anyway.'

I went back into the room to check on the player, who was unbelievably relieved and emotional. I told her she hadn't done anything wrong and to let me sort this out. I left her to rest, telling her to lock her door behind me.

I resolved not to tell the team or Kelly and Haley, our coaches, because we had to focus on the game. I didn't want to disrupt things; I wanted to work out a way to fix it. But the following morning at breakfast, while I was still trying to digest what I had seen and how I should best report it, a different player approached me while I stood at the buffet, and leant in close: 'Khalida, I'm going to say something to you, but don't react to what I say right here. Some of the players from Afghanistan are being pressured to go to the rooms of the two men with us. I know this because they've called me too and they've sent me texts. They want me to go to their room. It's getting worse and worse.' I listened carefully but kept my face neutral, my eyes sweeping the room to see if anyone was watching us. I knew she would get in trouble for passing on information, so we stood side by side helping ourselves to food as a cover for our conversation.

I didn't know what to do, how to balance handling the information sensitively whilst making sure players weren't being put in danger. Back in my room I received a text with a list of players who had been coerced into going to the coaches' room on previous nights. The person sending the message said she trusted me, that she had had to fight hard to be allowed to travel, and that getting permission from her parents had been extremely difficult. She warned me by saying what I already knew: that if the information was leaked back home, it would be hugely damaging. The players would be banned from school, work, football, and forced into marriages, into a life they had not chosen themselves. I knew it was true. I had seen it happen.

Later that day the team captain and another player approached me after a team meeting. They were agitated.

'Khalida, we left school to come here,' one of them explained. 'It was hard enough because of what people say to our families about us. We have not asked for any financial support, we have not asked for anything. We have given so much and these two men are taking advantage of the players and undermining it all. If my father finds out what I've come into, he will never trust me and will never let me play again. I can't go onto the pitch knowing what is going on.'

A few hours ahead of a training game I grabbed Kelly. I had to share what was going on. She didn't panic; she calmly absorbed the information. She is the kind of person you need in a crisis, because she breathes solutions and thinks about how to solve the problem. She has the rare talent of being able to make you feel confident that everything will be OK.

'We can – if you want, if you say so – put these two men on a plane and send them back to Afghanistan,' she said. 'If that is the solution, if that is what you want, I can do that.'

I said we should wait, speak to Karim and report it properly, while keeping these men away from the girls. Kelly, meanwhile, spoke to the players: 'We hear you. This is not acceptable for us. We would never want or allow this type of behaviour around our team, and we are going to find a solution as soon as possible.' We told the players they were not alone, and that we would fight for them and protect them.

I phoned Karim and Kelly switched focus to the game. Karim's response was rapid. He told me not to worry, that it was unacceptable and that he would call the coaches directly and get them removed. He reacted as he had done all those years ago in Germany. But then his tone changed suddenly, and he began to talk regretfully about the impact this news could have on the whole programme if it got out. How it could destroy the entire programme, and how our efforts would have been for nothing. I got the sense he was trying to scare me. Yet, he was conciliatory too: 'It's fine if the players do not wear the hijab, we should not force them,' he said. 'It's fine if they want to wear shorts, totally fine. They don't need to wear tights or a hijab. It should be optional.'

This was something that I had been fighting for for a long time, and suddenly he was agreeing to it. I felt like he was taking responsibility for that decision, so I delivered the news to the team. 'The hijab and base layers are optional. We've had permission from the president to choose,' I reported. The players were extremely happy, because they had been struggling in the oppressive heat and our game was scheduled for the middle of the afternoon.

We played the game and finished the tour without any further incidents. In our last meeting before the players would return to Afghanistan and I to Denmark, I stood in front of the team and I told them that we would continue to fight for them, that what had happened on this tour would never happen again.

I returned from the trip to Jordan to a new job with the Right to Dream Academy, an organisation that had started as a football academy based in Ghana and expanded to something far more ambitious, even buying the Danish football team FC Nordsjælland in 2015. I had attended a talk by their CEO, Tom Vernon, and was struck by their ambitions and their belief that football could change lives. I asked if I could intern with them as part of my master's, and later I was offered a job.

But though I was in a role that was perfect for me, I spent a big portion of my time on the phone to people in Afghanistan, trying to find out if Karim was delivering on what he had promised. I had given my word to the team and I couldn't let them down. Over the years, I had been forced to put my trust in Karim. Again and again, I had been given assurances that he would protect my sisters. Yet again, I was putting my trust in him.

15

A team is a relationship of trust. A dressing room is a sacred space. To betray that trust is unforgiveable. Open your eyes.

It was shortly after the training camp in Jordan that I began to discover the full extent of what was going on. While Karim did take action against the two coaches, he also ensured that nine players, including some of the country's best, were kicked off the team. They were accused of being lesbians, a hugely taboo thing in Afghanistan, which is extremely homophobic.

Accusing these players of being lesbians was a tactical move, as it killed their voices. Any association with them meant other players would be at risk, and their families would be in danger as a result too. The sidelining of nine players is what prompted me to investigate a little deeper. This wasn't a player here and there failing to show up; this was a mass exodus of players who didn't want to go.

I needed to find out how deeply this abuse extended, how many had suffered. So, I began to search for players, particularly those who had gone missing. Rumours were rife once I was in the know. One young player was believed to have given birth to Karim's child. When I spoke to women, I started to hear about sexual abuse, and physical abuse if they resisted. The Football Federation would come up with an excuse to get rid of them so that if they came out and spoke publicly, it would look like they were just upset at having been kicked off the team. I learnt for the first time that the women who had come to Germany with the coach in 2010 had been paid off and never heard from again.

I recorded story after story and started to collate them to build up a portfolio of evidence. There were five players prepared to go on record, so, armed with the knowledge of how systemic and extensive Karim's abuse was, I looked for a way to report it. There was no way of reporting it within the federation, as Karim was in complete control of everything going on within it. He was all-powerful. Outside the federation, there was nowhere to go either. Afghan society was not receptive to complaints about the abuse of women. It was a part of society, and the federation was a microcosm of that. The police couldn't be trusted to protect women, and neither could the courts, so I tried to find a way to report these abuses to the international footballing authorities instead.

Kelly worked with me to try and find a way. We approached the Asian Football Confederation and they essentially said: 'We can't speak to you about this because you're not a member of the association. We need your president or your general secretary to speak with us.'

We tried to explain that it was the president that our complaints were against, but they just said that was the procedure we had to follow. It was infuriating. It didn't make sense – the system was designed to protect the team's abuser.

We had similar trouble trying to reach out to FIFA, as there was no obvious formal way of reporting the most senior members of a federation safely. A joint conference held by FIFA and the Asian Football Confederation in April 2018 offered a window of opportunity to reach out to senior women within both organisations. One of those was FIFA's head of women's football, Sarai Bareman.

Kelly and I asked Sarai if she would speak to us about abuse suffered by members of the national team. She listened, and we connected with a small number of people within the organisation who worked quietly to investigate our claims, while trying to prevent word reaching Karim. I provided them with everything I knew. I arranged for them to speak to the players. I translated. I went back for more information when required. We waited and waited for FIFA to launch a formal investigation, but months went by.

Meanwhile, Kelly and I worked to try and help the five players who were prepared to go on record get out of the country. They were taking a huge risk by speaking to FIFA. We were struggling to get support for these women, many of whom were in hiding, and one of which was in a refugee camp in Turkey, so we paid for flights and hotels out of our own pockets to get some of them into Pakistan. It was only after we had done that that FIFA began to take over, arranging for the players to travel to Switzerland.

Still, the case against Karim had not been formally opened yet. Our frustrations were increasing. We feared FIFA would try to cover it up – not necessarily those working on the case, but others. We knew the value of the votes of member associations and how influential and important the allegiance of federations was. The longer we waited, the more paranoid we became about what was going on behind the scenes.

Then, one day, I was put in touch with *Guardian* journalist Suzanne Wrack. She had interviewed our captain, Shabnam Mobarez, nine months before and they had stayed in touch. When Shabnam, who was one of the players who lived outside the country, had tweeted about the new contracts that the Afghanistan Football Federation had told players to sign if they wanted to remain on the team, Suzanne reached out to ask what was happening. It was clear that the federation feared players speaking out, they feared further exposure of abuses. The federation was using new contracts to silence players or get rid of those who wouldn't keep quiet by stating that players couldn't be paid to play football at club level and were not permitted to secure individual sponsorship deals or pursue promotional ventures. It also removed the right to mediation in disciplinary proceedings.

Suzanne wanted to write about the contracts, but Shabnam and Mina Ahmadi, a player based in Germany, gave her the impression that there was more to the story than they were telling. Both separately encouraged her to speak to Kelly, their coach, for more details. It was Kelly who, for the first time, spoke frankly to Suzanne about the abuses I had uncovered. She explained that one of the barriers to players talking about the abuse was an inability to use the right language, because the language of abuse just didn't exist in Afghanistan. 'Abuse' wasn't a word that was in the vocabulary of the population, and neither was rape or sexual assault. These were things that women had to accept as part of life, not crimes.

Kelly put Suzanne in touch with me. I don't know why I trusted her, but I did. Possibly because she was clear from the start that there was no obligation for us to do a story together, that we could just talk about what was going on and discuss whether an article was worthwhile and possible.

After that first conversation, Suzanne was horrified by what she heard. We began the long task of gathering material for an article that would make the biggest impact. We went through the interview transcripts and began to piece a story together that would be published in the *Guardian* in December 2018. Again and again, we would hear how Karim would use players' vulnerabilities to force himself on them. One girl tentatively approached Karim's office after training one week to ask whether the federation could help with her travel costs. 'I asked for help,' she said. 'He started trying to come closer to me. He said: "I want to come closer to you, I want to see your body."'

I was repeating the words, translating them from Dari to English for Suzanne, yet at the same time I was trying to zone out of what was being said, to repeat individual, isolated words. It was easier to translate that way, emotionlessly. I had heard what had happened to this player already. I didn't want to hear it again, but I had to. She was speaking from a refugee camp in Turkey, trapped in the system, desperate to end her life and end the suffering. Speaking to the media was her last hope, but she could only do so under complete anonymity, for the safety of herself and her family.

> I tried to ignore him. I was very polite to him. I said: 'Listen, I need money for my transportation, I don't have money. Can you help me? If you can't, please let me go.' He said he would help me and told me to wait. I said I wanted to go home. He said: 'Don't worry, I will give you money.'
>
> The president told me to follow him to the next room. So, I went with him. I thought he was going to help me. He went into another room and there was another room off that, which was very dark. Inside that room there was a door. But you can't see the door; it looks like the wall. It is hard to see it's a door. It was open. In there it was like a hotel room, with a bedroom inside. It had everything, even a bathroom. He told me to go in. I went in. He was behind me, and he locked the door.
>
> He told me to sit on the bed. I was worried, I was shaking. He said: 'Today I want to find out what is underneath your clothes.'
>
> I told him to leave me alone, that I wanted to go home. I stood up and he said to me: 'Scream as much as you want, no one will hear you. They can't hear you.'
>
> Then he started pushing me towards the bed.
>
> I stood up again. I said: 'Leave me alone, I only came for help. Please leave me alone, let me go.'
>
> He was telling me . . . that today he would find out if I was a lesbian or not – because I was with girls a lot and I looked a little like a boy.

> I stood up and tried to fight, but he punched me in the face. I fell onto the bed. I tried to get up and go to the door, but it was not possible to open it without his fingerprint. So I couldn't get out. He punched me in the face and on my mouth. Blood was coming from my nose and lips. He started beating me. I fell onto the bed and everything went dark . . .
>
> When I woke up, all my clothes were off and there was blood everywhere. I was shaking. I didn't know what had happened to me. The bed was covered in blood; blood was coming from my mouth, nose and vagina. I went to the bathroom. I washed my face and put my clothes on. I went back and said: 'I will go like this and I will tell the media what happened to me.'
>
> He took a gun, his gun, put it against my head and said: 'See what I have done to you? I can shoot you in the head and your brains will be everywhere. And I can do the same with your family. If you want your family to be alive, you should keep quiet.'
>
> Then he threw money at my face and told me to take it and get out. He said he didn't want to see my face. He opened the door and I left.

She ran to a friend's house. She couldn't go home; she couldn't tell her family what had happened. Her friend gently cleaned her bloodied face and helped her wash and dress in clean clothes so she could face her family. She told them a less-than-convincing story of having suffered a sporting injury, safe in the knowledge that her parents would believe it, because they would be too scared to think otherwise. Her ordeal was far from over:

> I did not feel well. I found out through friends in the team that the president had spread a rumour that I was a lesbian –

> that he had caught me with another girl and that was why I was kicked out. That was depressing and very dangerous for me . . . I know that my family is in danger, and I know they will be when more comes out. But I want to stand and speak about it because of the future of girls. I want girls to have a safe environment.

A second player told me she was asked to go to Karim's office by another member of the federation. 'I was not aware of his character,' she said. She walked into his office and Karim gestured for her to sit on the sofa in the corner. Then he hulked himself from behind his desk and sat down next to her. 'He started talking and flirting with me. He started touching my body and then he tried to kiss me. I started crying. I was scared and I was panicking. I was trying to push him away.'

She screamed and lashed out, trying to claw at him and twist away. She fled the building, struck by how little attention was paid to her as she left, crying and broken. She didn't return for more than a month, instead staying hidden, hoping that if she vanished the problem would vanish. 'I was feeling so weak and I couldn't share my story. At the same time, I was receiving phone calls from the federation, and especially from the president, pushing me, pressuring me to come back because it was destroying his image.'

Eventually, she relented, but all she had done in escaping was fuel Karim's desire for her. 'Whenever I went to training, the president would come to the pitch and in front of everyone say I was not polite and talked too much. He would directly threaten me, saying he would cut out my tongue to silence me. He was abusing and harassing me non-stop.'

One day she was early for training at the federation:

> I was sitting on the benches waiting for the rest of the team. He saw I was there on the security cameras. He

started calling me on the phone. I was ignoring it, so he came out himself and told me to come. I had to follow him; there was nothing I could do. I had to pass through four doors – he had gone ahead and had me on the phone giving me instructions of where to go.

After the four doors I was in a bedroom. It was like a five-star hotel with a mirror, modern furniture, a bed and women's perfumes on the drawers. When I got there and saw that, I started recalling the stories I had heard . . . I was scared and I started crying, I thought it was the end of my life.

The president was naked and was on the bed, waiting for me. When I started crying he got up and ran towards me and held me. He tried to pull my scarf and dress away. He was attacking me and tearing at my clothes. I was crying, screaming, struggling. I was very lucky: he received a phone call and when he answered it, I started screaming. He pushed me away and tried to silence me, but I didn't stop screaming. He had no choice then, and he opened the door. When he opened the door I ran.

Another player went to Karim's office to get his signature on a document when her ordeal started:

I was trying to push him away and he was trying to kiss my neck and lips. I was telling him to behave and that he was the age of my grandfather and how could he do it? He told me he didn't know why I was behaving weird with him, that I was so friendly with him outside.

I said I thought he was just a friend. He was very social and he told me that 'Our friendship is having sex at the end.' I said: 'I hate to even hear these things. Let me go.' I was trying to push him away and I ran from the room.

> The first thing he did was take me off the list of the national team for a training camp abroad. Then he insulted me in front of everyone and accused me of being a lesbian and kicked me out of the federation.'

I would finish each session with Suzanne almost unable to speak, overcome with anger, horror and sadness. Tom Vernon and the Right to Dream team were incredible for allowing me the space to do this work. They divided up my work and gave it to others to allow me to focus. And slowly, piece by piece, we began to establish the story.

The picture of Karim that emerged was of a man with two wives and eleven known children. He was a man who had used women's football to bring young vulnerable women into his lustful orbit. And I had helped him. I tried to tell myself that I had been operating outside the country, that I was not there day to day to see what was taking place. The president of the Football Federation had turned the organisation into his own personal non-consensual brothel. And I had been the one bringing women into it.

Everything made sense now: the players who had gone missing and those who had replaced them had been pawns in his personal game. He had worked hard to convince me not to speak out publicly on the abuse by the coaches, not for the sake of women's football but to maintain his hustle. I felt stupid, naive and manipulated, but most of all I was crippled with guilt. I had handed these women to Karim. I had wanted to free them, to open their eyes to the opportunities that were out there for women, to empower them. Instead I had pulled them into a place of abuse. I felt fiercely determined to right that wrong, to avenge and look after those harmed, and to protect current and future players who had yet to be targeted by this man, who felt himself to be invincible.

Suzanne and I worked together tirelessly for over two months to get the story to a point where it could be published. It was hard, because we couldn't prove definitively that rape and abuse had taken place. Instead, we had to build up a sufficiently convincing picture, backed up by evidence that would never be published, to ensure the article was legally as sound as it could be. I will always be grateful to the *Guardian*, because they believed in us and in trying to create change.

'There was blood everywhere.'

That was the headline. My hands shook as I scrolled through the article on the *Guardian*'s website, published on 27 December 2018. It had been months of work and the story had dominated my life for over a year. There had been no outlet for us – no one would listen – but the publication of this article finally dropped a bomb on the Football Federation building that sent shockwaves through the country and across the world. I breathed deeply. There were huge risks involved. I read the article again. I had already read it. I had already combed it for any identifying features of the five players, but I needed to look again. I needed to make sure, as much as I could, that Karim wouldn't be able to tell who had spoken out.

The trauma, fear and despair of the players tumbled from the screen into my soul. I knew what they had said; I had heard their stories. But seeing their voices in black and white – and watching on social media as the number of retweets, quote tweets and likes mounted up by the second and the news was picked up all over the world – was indescribable.

The impact of the article was huge. Kelly, Shabnam, Mina and I all spoke out about what had been going on, detailing the events at the camp in Jordan and demanding action. It made an impact inside and outside of Afghanistan. The attorney general's office in the country announced an investigation into the allegations. Jamshid Rasooli, a spokesman for the attorney general's office, said: 'This committee has been created after the *Guardian* newspaper published a report about abuse and sexual mistreatment against members of the Afghanistan women's football team. This committee will investigate the case and will seriously act, according to law, with people who are involved.' The president of the country, Ashraf Ghani, also commented: 'Unfortunately, despite our achievements, international media have had some kind of allegations regarding the Football Federation which the *Guardian* newspaper and international TV stations have focused on. This is shocking for all the people of Afghanistan. No kind of disrespect against our boy and girl athletes is acceptable. I want the attorney general to investigate this thoroughly. I cannot tolerate immorality.' FIFA also formally announced their investigation.

But the narrative was being shifted by the Football Federation and Karim's people. In Afghanistan, we were painted as meddling foreigners with an axe to grind. It was at that stage that the players impacted decided to tell their stories, to kill that line and redirect the focus back onto Karim. That prompted FIFA to suspend Karim and four other members of the federation, and they were issued with travel bans by the government.

In June 2019, seven months after the first article was published – and in a week during which I helped the *Guardian* expose the fact that senior officials within the Asian Football Confederation and FIFA had been made aware of possible sexual abuse, corruption and the abuse of a fourteen-year-old boy as early as April 2017 – FIFA made an announcement. Karim was banned for life from all football-related activity and fined one million Swiss francs:

> In its decision, the adjudicatory chamber found that Mr Karim had breached article 23 (protection of physical and mental integrity) and article 25 (abuse of position) of

> the FIFA code of ethics and sanctioned him with a life ban from all football-related activities (administrative, sports or any other) at both national and international level.

Despite an arrest warrant being issued in Afghanistan too, Karim remained, and remains, at large. An arrest attempt in August 2020 was blocked by a supportive militia in the province where he had been a governor. He remains at large, having evaded the criminal justice system, but the world knows his crimes against women.

16

Copenhagen, August 2021

An orchestra isn't an orchestra if everyone plays the same instrument and a team won't survive or thrive without people with a multitude of different skills. Open your eyes.

The phone was buzzing. I lifted my head from the desk, fumbled for it clumsily. It was an unknown number. A voice was whispering, hoarse.

'Is that Khalida?' said a woman, speaking in Dari.

'Yes.' My throat was dry. I rubbed my eyes, unsure if I was still dreaming.

'I have my brother's gun. I am sitting in front of my window, watching outside. I have not slept. When they knock on my door, I will shoot myself in my head. It is better to kill myself than be caught by them.'

I knew then that this was not a dream.

I tapped a key on the keyboard and my screen flared to life. My screensaver was a team photograph, taken ten years ago, when it still felt like we were at the beginning of something. We were all smiling. We had hope then, back when that picture was taken. But hope felt very far away now.

Over the next day, WhatsApp informed me three times in one day that I had reached maximum capacity for receiving incoming calls or messages. Friends, family, former teammates and players I worked with were sending me messages. But so were players who I didn't know, in their teens and early twenties, girls and women who had begun playing long after I had left Afghanistan ten years before. Girls and women who had not experienced life under the Taliban. They were frightened. They knew that they were targets.

When I was not listening to messages or answering calls, I would send emails to everyone I had ever met in the world of sport: 'Please. Whatever you can do, help me help them.'

My hands were shaking with caffeine and adrenaline. I stood up, but felt suddenly faint and collapsed back into my chair. If I could just sleep for longer than ten minutes. After the article on Karim's abuse of the players was published in 2018 there had been a huge explosion of media interest, but that had since faded away. I had made peace with that. My role in Afghan football would be at one remove, through organising our 'Girl Power' football programmes.

I put my head down and closed my eyes.

'Khalida?'

I awoke with a start to Russ knocking on the office door, his face concerned. The office was dark. I had fallen asleep again at my desk.

'It's late. Come on, let's go home.'

As we drove though the Copenhagen night, under the soft orange of the streetlights, I began to cry. Gently at first, trying to hold the tears in. But then louder and louder, until I was sobbing, unable to breathe. Russ quietly pulled the car over and sat in silence, watching me. When I could speak, I was almost shouting.

'It's my fault. If I hadn't done this . . . if we hadn't made them believe they could play . . . if I hadn't smiled for all those photographs with all of these people who wanted to associate themselves with girls playing football in Afghanistan. And now where are they? Not a single one will answer my calls, or they tell me there's nothing they can do. Meanwhile, the West is telling the story that we have surrendered to the Taliban. I have family in the army that have been begging to fight back. They betrayed us and now they are blaming us for it. They have no shame. I have so many messages from hundreds of girls who need help, but nobody is listening.'

Russ didn't say anything. He knew me well enough by now. He knew I needed the space where I could be myself. I heard my family's voices in my head: 'Why should we fight for you if you're not willing to fight for yourself?' I took a deep breath.

That night, as Russ cooked dinner, I sat and I wrote a post on LinkedIn. I told the story of my family fleeing Afghanistan when the Taliban took power. I spoke about how it was happening again, and how the world was turning its back on the women and girls of Afghanistan. Western forces were leaving in the middle of the night, leaving their feel-good speeches behind them. Now women were dying. Women were being raped. Schools were burning.

All of those things my generation had believed when we returned to Afghanistan: that we could change things, that we could build a new future for the next generation of girls, a future of education, opportunity and participation in art and culture and sport. Now I knew it was all bullshit. Now there was no right to dream. Now that the Taliban were back in power, it seemed that each nation was trying to get their own people out of Afghanistan as quickly as possible, with little regard for the plight of others, let alone Afghans. Meanwhile women and girls were being taken by the Taliban for sex slaves. I had hundreds of messages from women and girls who were terrified, begging for help. But I was helpless.

In Denmark, I was once told by a man in the street to 'fuck off back home' to my own country. How could I have explained, back then, that I no longer had a home? And now, no longer any hope? I poured all of my frustration, anger and sadness into my words. I pressed 'send' and went to bed.

I was woken by my phone vibrating intermittently on the table next to my bed. I lay there for a moment, enjoying the feeling of coming out of the deepest sleep that I had experienced in a long time. I heard the shower being turned off, the traffic of the distant city. Russ put his head around the door, his hair wet and sticking to his head.

'I think you'd better take a look at your post.'

Overnight, my post had been shared thousands of times. There were comments left by people from around the world – messages of support, sorrow and anger. When I checked my emails I saw message after message offering support from those I had met over the years, including international human rights lawyer Kat Craig and our former coach Kelly Lindsey. They all wanted to know what they could do, how they could help. Good questions, I thought.

Then there was one from Jonas Baer-Hoffmann, the general secretary of FIFPRO, the international union that represents the interests of footballers around the world. It had one question: 'How do we get them out?'

I gave him an honest answer, which was that I had no idea. The Taliban controlled the borders, so the only way out was by air. I didn't have a plane, or money. I didn't know politicians or anyone with influence. My world was sport.

'Let me talk to some people,' Jonas said.

Along with Kat and Kelly, we began to form a plan. Jonas leant on his networks. He spoke to people in Germany and Belgium. He reached out to politicians within his network, and he started to connect us to anyone he could think of who could be useful. The plan was to find a country that would accept the fleeing players. We might not know how to get them out, but there were things we could do. So we started to find those who could provide asylum to them, started to work out what documents we needed, how we needed to apply.

Kat told me to get documents from the players – whatever they could find that proved they were a player, whatever identification they could get together. That was thrilling, but also terrifying, because I had to contact the players and ask them for those things without giving them false hope. I had to tell them that I had no idea how to help them and that I couldn't make any promises, but that we would try our best to help and support them. They had been given so much false hope for so many years, only to be betrayed. I knew I could not add to that.

We had between twenty-four and forty-eight hours to maybe – just maybe – get people onto planes. We had no idea how those hours would unfold, what would change or develop. Consequently, there was no slowing down. Time was of the essence and the clock was ticking. We decided together to treat every twenty-four hours as though it was the last, and to do as much as we could.

Kat managed practical things like documentation and Kelly helped with the bigger picture, the process: why a player needs to leave, who is in danger and why, what is needed, what would happen if she stayed in Afghanistan. Kat Blu-tacked a handwritten sign saying 'London evacuation HQ' above her dining-room table. There she compiled lists of names and what documents we had for them. Several times she said we just couldn't take any more, but Kelly would just slide in and say, 'Go on, just this one more person.' It wasn't that anyone wanted to leave people out; it was just that our capacity to help was limited. We had been told by FIFA that they were 'monitoring the situation', but the window in which there was access in and out of the airport in Kabul was closing rapidly while they 'monitored'. We were already trying to make the impossible possible, and Kelly just pushed us to increase the size of what impossible looked like.

We were working like the fingers on one hand, each with a different role, coming together as a big strong punch to try to evacuate players and people connected to them from the Hamid

Karzai International Airport. We created what became known as 'the List'. It was really a succession of various lists, as we tried to work out who was at greatest risk and how to get them out first. It was a triage system.

'Kat,' I said, frantic. 'I can't do this, how can we judge who is most at risk?'

'Well,' said Kat, 'the way I see it, sometimes if you wait to do a perfect thing, you won't do the good thing.' So that became our guiding light. We would do what we could because at least it was doing something.

Through connections to the US military through Haley, we were able to get information in real time about movements of the Taliban and military personnel on the ground. And thus we eventually pulled off what seemed completely impossible: to get a group of female football players, many of them teenagers, and a host of others, including family members, into the airport and onto planes.

There were three groups of players: the senior women's national team, one of the youth teams, and a group which included players from the Herat provincial team, from some of the other provincial teams and from some clubs. The national team was mainly located in Kabul but they came from different provinces, as those selected for the senior national team had moved to the capital. They had held their last training session two weeks before the fall of Kabul. I had to tell the players to keep hiding, to stay on the move while we got going.

We tracked everything. Kat scoured human rights and women's equality groups and even reached out to former military personnel she had previously faced in the courtroom. Jonas kept pulling on every connection through FIFPRO that he could, and we all watched out for announcements from governments who were evacuating people other than their own citizens to identify countries that Kat, Jonas and others could focus their efforts on. We started with a list of the four most vulnerable players – the ones who had been the most vocal about women's rights and who would be the biggest targets for the Taliban.

The US, Canada, Belgium, Germany, the UK and Australia were all countries we managed to persuade to add our players' names to their evacuation lists within the first twenty-four hours. We got to the stage where we were confident enough that we could contact the players and tell them to head to the airport in Kabul.

A major turning point in our efforts was connecting with a group in Australia who were also working with athletes trapped in the country. The former Olympian and human rights lawyer Nikki Dryden, who Kat knew, and the director of Human Rights for All, Alison Battisson, joined our little team. They brought in former Socceroo Craig Foster, who had led the campaign to save Bahraini footballer Hakeem al-Araibi from detention in Thailand in 2019. Through them, we were fast-tracked to the right people in the Australian government to advocate asylum for as many players as possible. Through another former Olympian and member of the Australian parliament, Zali Steggall, we were able to get visa applications in for athletes. Alison lodged multiple immigration cases and Zali provided a cover letter. Our plan was that players would get to the gates of the airport and show the letters from Zali, FIFPRO and FIFA to prove they were legitimately at risk, but we didn't know if it would work.

Once we managed to get players onto lists, we needed to reach the senior military and government personnel who could bump the players up the list. This was very difficult for us, because what makes one woman's life more valuable than any other's? But our most high-profile players were probably some of the most at-risk women in the country, and the national team was particularly at risk.

★

I coached the players over the phone.

'Wear the niqab. Cover up completely. Keep your documents in your underwear. Split up your money and hide it in different places. If the Taliban stop you at a checkpoint, tell them your husband is on the other side and he'll be angry if you don't get to him. Get into a panic about your husband getting angry with you.'

Fortunately, Haley had served two tours of Iraq with the US Marines so she reached out to some of her military contacts, veterans who knew what was happening on the ground in real time. Through satellite images and intelligence, these contacts were able to share information with us about where the Taliban checkpoints were. We worked out that the best time to get through the checkpoints was between 3 and 4 a.m., but there were thousands of people trying to get through.

Once through the checkpoints, attempting to get players inside the airport became key. Eventually, Haley used her connections to reach three key soldiers – an Australian, a Briton and an American – who were at the airport. We were sending messages to players throughout the night, telling them when the guards would change, after which it would be the British on the ground. We gave them details of the contact and then told them to fight to get to the front, to work together.

The players spent three days at the airport. They fought so hard to get into the building. The first day, it didn't happen. Many had travelled there with their families and I had to tell them that we couldn't help to get families out, that the visas were only for the football players. We had to encourage them to leave their families behind, but in the end we had to allow them to make that decision for themselves. I told them that if they wanted to try to get their families out too with the letters they had, then they could give it a go, but I reminded them not to make any promises to their families, just as I was making no promises to them. We couldn't promise anything; we left that fight to them. I knew that whatever route they chose they would always blame themselves and carry the burden of guilt.

The conditions were horrific: a crush of thousands of desperate people, with more arriving every minute, desperate to be allowed into the airport. Some of the players were beaten. Some were with small children or younger siblings who couldn't endure those conditions, so they gave up and went home. Some tried to find ways into the airport but couldn't. One group had to climb into a sewer to avoid a patrol.

We managed to get the first plane with our players on it on the runway. We had their names on the list, and the Australian authorities were waiting for them. I paced around the living room, unable to sit down. Any minute, I thought, I would get a call saying a van with the Taliban inside had arrived, dragged our players off the plane, beaten them, dragged them back.

My phone rang. It was Kat.

'The plane is in the air!' she cried.

'And they're on it?'

'Everyone on the flight list.'

We immediately had a meeting call with the extended group that had worked to get the team out.

'I'm not done, not till the last day of the evacuation,' I said. 'This is not a time for celebration for me yet, we're not done.'

As the hours seeped by, we were able to get more names on our list, and more players onto flight lists. One player, Fatima Yousoufi, the goalkeeper, made it onto a flight list, but her younger sibling didn't. Her family told her to go. She got on the plane not knowing what would happen to her. We worked the whole day, using selfies of them, tracing them with grid references, contacting the authorities with copies of their passports. I explained how vulnerable the families of these girls were. We got Fatima's sibling onto another plane five minutes before it lifted off the tarmac. Then we spent the entire time the flight was in the air sorting out their visa applications. She only knew we'd managed to get her sibling out when they walked towards her in Dubai airport.

But then, on 26 August, there was the first suicide bomb.

I got a call from one of the players who had been left outside the airport. 'They've welded the airport gates shut. No one is getting out. There was an explosion. It's chaos here.'

'What about our girls? Did they make it out?'

No one had any information. I paced around the room, waiting for an update. The players still there had been part of the Herat provincial team that won the domestic league and had been photographed with President Ghani and their trophy. They were high risk.

Minutes blurred into hours. The suicide bomb created panic. People were trying to get into the airport and out of the country quicker. Women were pushed, harassed and physically injured, because the men trying to escape knew that women would be prioritised if they got to the front. Many men tried everything possible to stop women from making it to the front. They were touching their bodies, grabbing them and trying to force them back.

Amid this chaos, the players banded together and used the men in their families as shields. They formed human circles, with the men around groups of girls clustered together, and in those groups they pushed through the crowds together. But getting to the front of the queue was just another hurdle. Over and over they pushed, only to reach the gate and find it closed, so they had to move on to the next one.

Some of the players were stuck outside in a queue. They couldn't even get into the airport as tens of thousands of desperate Afghans crowded around the entrance.

'You have to push to the front,' I told one of the players over the phone. 'Get your biggest defender and your quickest winger and use strength to push through. You have to get to the front.' They were being beaten.

We were informed that the Taliban were out there in the crowds around the airport, with electric cattle prods. Time was running out. I called one of the players again to tell them to get to the front. Kelly took hold of the phone and shouted, 'You are fucking champions! This is the time to go. You have to push! You gotta do everything you can to get there!' They eventually made it to the front, and I have no doubt Kelly's motivation helped them to get there.

Every now and again, someone would say that their papers weren't valid and we would all scramble to tell them to not leave, to not give up, to fight for themselves and to keep talking. I used Kelly's old coaching pick-me-ups: 'Together unbreakable, we can do this, we can be champions!' I was living all her speeches and texting people: 'One team, one unit! Passion, pride, never quit, go go go, you can do it!'

Some of our players were only sixteen, seventeen, eighteen years old. Some spent three nights outside the airport in the hands of the Taliban. Some were stuck at the checkpoints. They were scared. They were beaten with guns and whips, across their heads, bodies and faces. Some of them were badly injured. Some had the Taliban shooting at them. But throughout all of this, my role was to reassure them that there was hope and there were people trying to help them.

'No matter what,' I would say, 'we will not leave anyone behind. Stay strong, do not give up. We will do everything possible to stay as a team.'

In those moments, I didn't give a shit about football, because these were life-and-death situations and innocent lives, but I was telling them: 'This is a football game. We are in the Champions League, we are in the final, we're going to win this! For us, for this moment, our trophy is to get to the gate.' The language of football was something we all understood and I knew it would resonate enough to give them the strength and motivation to succeed against the odds.

The rules to get into the airport kept changing. Suddenly a pending visa was not enough; it had to be approved. Suddenly unaccompanied minors needed parental consent, despite some having lost both their parents. It was hurdle after hurdle after hurdle, but we just kept going, and the hours were slowly disappearing.

The longer it went on, the more we had to encourage the players to send their families home. It was getting increasingly difficult to get players out, let alone their large families. Those were tough conversations. The women and girls had pushed and waited. They were starved of food and water. They had held on until they were almost there and then we were telling them to leave their children, their sisters or mothers. It was heartbreaking. Yet they knew, as we did, that it was the only way.

There was so much going on and things were changing so quickly it was difficult to keep up. Phone calls were fleeting, and the signal was bad, so the audio often cut out or crackled so much that words were incoherent. It was chaos. Some of the girls got out and some of them were turned away, but we didn't know which.

My phone rang. The Herat team were alive, but they had been taken off a Qatari-supported bus at the last minute, sacrificed for a group of lawyers, policewomen and others who took their place, with more senior people advocating for them. It was a game of chess: all the pieces were at risk, but my sisters had been demoted to pawn status, and could therefore be sacrificed.

I slumped into my seat for a moment. Then I sat up. We just had to find a different plan.

I knew I couldn't let them know that hope was also draining from me. They were broken. They had come so close; sitting on the bus they had started to believe they would be safe, only to be dragged back into danger.

I video-called them. They were sitting on the floor, many of them crying, hopeless. They were giving up. 'I don't have the energy in my legs to move,' said the player on the other end of my call.

'You have to,' I said. 'You have to keep going.'

I was at my mum's flat. I put the phone down, lay on her bed, and cried. I cried and cried until my eyes hurt because there was no moisture left to make more tears.

The players had to make their way back to Kabul, with their families in tow – families who had trusted them, and me. They were left roaming the streets of the capital, trying to find somewhere to stay. The players and their families made up a group of around a hundred and thirty people, trying to hide who they were and what they were doing while the city swarmed with Taliban forces. It was very difficult to find them somewhere to stay, and I had to lean heavily on contacts in Kabul, friends and people I trusted. I couldn't send money across to help – the banks had been shut down – so the families had to sell everything they had: they took off their jewellery and put together the few possessions they had managed to travel with in order to pay for somewhere to stay and food to eat. They didn't all know each other either. They were from different provinces, so regional and ethnic tensions were fraught. Some of the girls' families were losing faith in the idea of leaving, saying that it had been a mistake.

All my muscles felt tense, stretched beyond breaking point, by the feeling of responsibility to these women and their families. I was not in the country. I was not living it. I was just giving advice over the phone, and the weight of that was heavy. There were no guarantees. I had to be so careful not to make any promises, as I wouldn't be able to bear it if they felt lied to. I didn't know what to say to the Herat players who had been taken off the coach. What could I write? 'I'm sorry, I tried. I can't help you?' I was crippled with pain at the thought of it.

Instead, I tried to stay positive: 'It's good you're not at the airport. You're alive. I don't know what the next steps are; I don't know what the plan is, but let's find a way. Let me think, give me time.' But I was lost. I had no idea what to do.

On top of everything, there were tensions between some of the organisations involved with the evacuation plans, as they all wanted to be central to the story of getting women out of Afghanistan. There was talk of documentary crews and media deals, even before all of the women were safe. I felt this was dangerous and morally compromised, because these were extremely vulnerable women who were navigating a deeply traumatic time, not to mention the effects this would continue to have on them later as they processed the stress and grief. They deserved time and space for that delicate journey before deciding if they wanted to do interviews and have their names and faces forever associated with their trauma. Their stories were being sold without their consent. A similar process had played out with the national team: everyone involved wanted their hero moment, keen to place themselves and their role in rescuing the players front and centre in press releases and interactions with the media. I found that incredibly difficult to deal with, because it was championing those who had helped rather than these brave and strong women who had fought for their survival. The women were the real heroes. They didn't need saving – they were saving themselves – and that was the story that needed to be told, when they were ready, if they ever would be.

We had a list of players that I had compiled with the help of other players, officials and whatever documentation the players themselves could provide to prove their status. But each organisation coming on board had their own lists, their own connections, people they wanted to get out.

I called Kelly in tears. 'What if we got it wrong? What if there were others who we should have got out but didn't? What if our list was in the wrong order?'

'Khalida?' I heard her breathing on the other end of the phone. 'Do you remember, I always told our players to be brave? What I meant by that was that there's always an easy option. The safe pass. It's always easier not to take a penalty. But that doesn't win you the game. It might not work. We'll never know if we made the right choices. But I can tell you this with a hundred per cent certainty: you took the brave pass.'

There was a breakthrough when we managed to get the support of the Pakistan Football Federation with obtaining visas, making up a training camp and getting the girls through the border without passports. ROKiT (one of many organisations that volunteered to assist) covered the cost of the bus to get them to the border and across. But once they were across, control of the bus fell into the hands of the ex-president of the Pakistan Football Federation, a very powerful military man, Sardar Naveed. They were uncontactable. Their internet access was down and I couldn't communicate with them.

The plan had been that the team would travel to Islamabad, but they were rerouted to Lahore. They were holed up in a dangerous and scary place. When one of the players managed to get some internet access, they phoned me instantly.

'We have no idea what is going on since we got off the bus.' She was scared, I could hear it in her shaky voice. 'There's media all over us, taking photos and videos of us, asking questions, grabbing our families, taking photos of young children without even asking. We don't know what is happening, but there are so many people.'

I went onto social media and found videos and photos of the team all over the Pakistan Football Federation's accounts. Politicians in Pakistan were taking note too, and that was scary, because we didn't want the players to become pawns when we didn't yet have a country to move them on to. They were at risk and the exposure was huge. The Taliban were present in

Pakistan too; it was not a safe place. There was political unrest in Lahore, with demonstrations, strikes and battles between the Taliban and Pakistan government.

There was no protection for the players. They had no control over where they could go or what they could do. I had no control over what was happening to them either. I was gripped by fear, panicked. It was so dangerous, and I didn't know how to deal with the situation. They were lodged in a hostel where they had no privacy. There were gunmen everywhere, they told me, and journalists and photographers would come and go as they pleased, walking into the players' rooms uninvited and taking photos.

The players were terrified of saying the wrong thing to the wrong person, saying something about the Taliban that would provoke them, or something that would prompt Pakistan to send them back to Afghanistan. I was phoning Naveed constantly, losing my cool. We had asked the Pakistan Football Federation to help with letters to get the girls into the country, and instead they had lost control of their lives. It was disturbing.

'You have put them in grave danger by bringing in the media. What was the purpose of it? We don't have a country for them; will the Pakistani government take responsibility?'

'This is how it is,' he said.

He told me to get a sponsor to pay the costs of the hostel they had been put in. But the conditions were horrific. Perhaps due to the media presence, they weren't able to leave, open windows or even go onto the rooftop for some fresh air. Instead, they were essentially locked inside for nearly two months. Some of them started to get skin diseases due to the humidity and lack of natural light. Others became very unwell. Two or three family members of some of the players had severe mental health problems, and one tried to commit suicide.

I switched tactics with Naveed. I needed to be friendly with him, to form a connection.

'What these girls need,' I said to him, 'is a protector. Someone with broad shoulders who can shield them for the horror they've experienced.'

I tried being nice, kind, apologetic even. I was being political, trying to curry favour, to get him onside. It was like playing a role, a game, all to maintain a connection with the team and to try and move them out of this situation. But it was exhausting. I was so unbelievably tired and I struggled to stay in character, to not lose my temper and keep my emotions in check.

By that point we had also made contact with Leeds United chairman Andrea Radrizzani. I had to appeal to him to sponsor the players' accommodation and medical costs until we could get a government on board to offer the players visas. He was incredibly helpful, doing an interview with the BBC that helped us put pressure on the UK government to take the players. He said publicly that if the government provided visas then Leeds United would help support the players, help with their integration process and provide football opportunities for them.

The team's temporary visas were running out, and so was our time. News of leaders of the Taliban holding meetings in Pakistan was everywhere, and the players were stuck in the country and panicking.

I rang Kat. 'Can you help? The players are going to get sent back.'

She put me in contact with someone at the UNHCR. When the UK government confirmed they would provide visas for the players, relief welled up in me. Meanwhile, Naveed was demanding the UK government take financial responsibility for the players immediately.

I stayed consistent and continued fighting. 'We will not take care of any costs in Pakistan. They have to pay for Covid tests. They have to pay for the hostel. They have to pay for the flight. We will not find a flight for them,' Naveed was saying.

Our biggest issue was finding a flight to bring the team to the UK. I asked Andrea for help, as he was assisting with many of the other costs via his foundation Play for Change, and he connected me with Qatar Airways and another airline. But nobody responded. We had a few days to get the players out before their visas expired, and no way of doing it.

Then we had only 120 hours. I was running out of options, and I was running out of time. I called one of our partners, the Tzedek Association.

'I need your help,' I said. 'I'm in an awful situation. I'm so terrified. I'm so tired. I've been dealing with a lot of drama so far, a lot of politics.'

'What do you want from us?' they said.

'A chartered plane,' I replied, 'for next week, no later than Wednesday . . . and I need a confirmation by tomorrow.'

We went back and forth a little about the details, but they called me a few hours later and asked, 'What do you think about Kim Kardashian being a partner?'

All I wanted was to get the players out and to safety. If Kim Kardashian was able to help, then I would take it. 'Yes, please,' I told them.

They went away for a meeting, came back and said: 'Kim Kardashian is on board. She will sponsor a charter from Pakistan to bring the team to the UK.'

We got the date for the charter and I video-called the players. 'I have news for you: we got a chartered plane. You're leaving Pakistan. You will be free.' They were all crying, one of them videoed their reactions: dancing, crying, screaming, they were crazy. I was so relieved to finally hear joy in their voices.

Over the weeks and months that followed, there was a scramble by some people to position themselves at the centre of what had happened. There were those who questioned the status of the women we helped to get out, who suggested that others should have escaped in their place. But those of us who were there know what happened.

I was drinking tea with my mother and father in the kitchen of the small flat they both now called home. We had been able to bring my father to join us. The years had worn down his broad shoulders, but we still teased him for preening like a teenager.

My phone started buzzing. An unknown number.

'Is that Khalida?'

'Yes.'

'I called you before, in August. I was the one with my brother's gun.'

'I remember.'

'Well, I just wanted to say, I got out. My sister too. We got out.'

I was gripping the phone so tightly my knuckles were pale. There were tears in my eyes.

'I wanted just to say thank you,' she said. 'Thank you.'

Epilogue

Melbourne, August 2023

The story about Afghanistan's exiled women footballers was picked up by the world's media. Neither the Afghanistan Football Federation nor FIFA has spoken up for Afghanistan's women footballers. There hasn't been a single statement expressing sorrow or support for this dedicated group of players who have lost their dreams and their futures – and, in many cases, have had their families torn apart.

And still the men's team plays on. It has held training camps in Dubai and Tajikistan and is running as close to normal as is possible. We have no knowledge of what has happened to the budget for women's football. Is that money still going from FIFA to the federation and if it is: how is it being spent and what checks are in place? Football governance is a brotherhood, controlled and run overwhelmingly by men looking to maintain and extend their power, profile and personal wealth. Voting power is hugely valuable. Losing the allegiance of voting FIFA members is not an option considered by those at the top. That is why the Football Federation has been allowed to continue, to all extents and purposes unchecked. That is why they have felt able to court the Taliban and sideline women, because their vote in FIFA elections is valuable. What message does this send to women and girls around the world?

The World Cup in 2023 was one of struggle. Zambia, South Africa, Jamaica, England, the US, France and Spain were just some of the countries where players were forced to take action against abusive coaches; for equal pay – for any pay; for bonuses; for better conditions and more. It breaks my heart that the very moment that the Spanish team should have been celebrating their great victory, it was tarnished by men in positions of power.

I watched the Australia v. England semi-final and the England v. Spain final alongside my sisters. The World Cup made us feel like we were part of a movement, of something bigger. None of these players or struggles are connected in a literal sense, but on a grander scale it's all connected, always. Seeing women's football moving, developing and breaking records, you couldn't help but feel a part of those victories. The players on the pitch weren't just representing themselves and their countries – they represented every woman who has fought to play or wanted to play. We saw our energy in them. We saw them as leaders, representing us on the world stage. The world was watching women's football. The attention was on women, and being a part of that was very special.

I was desperate to take the team into the fan zones and pubs as well as the stadiums, so they could experience the positivity and joy emanating around the tournament. We had played against the odds, against so much negativity, and this was an antidote to it. Seeing a man grab his son's or daughter's hand, running to the stadium to make kick-off, or a man frustrated with a referee's call or a misplaced pass – these were incredible to witness first-hand. You could feel the change. It was the first time the national team players had experienced it on that scale for themselves. I had felt it once before, with the team based in England during the women's Euros the preceding year, and I wanted this team to feel it too. Their faces were a picture of childlike wonder. They didn't watch the football so much as they watched the people. When Sam Kerr scored in the semi-final, the feeling was electric. The country rose together, united in a shared joy, the players on either side of me screaming with them.

I feel a great responsibility to every woman and girl in Afghanistan who ever kicked a ball as a result of my work. I feel like I was played and used, and that is the most horrible, tumultuous feeling. I fought for women's football to exist, I fought for spaces for them to play, I fought for them to embrace something new, to find their strength. I laboured under the impression that we did so with a degree of relative safety. Logically, I know that this is not my fault, but logic doesn't always dominate. Instead, the knowledge that if I hadn't driven and pushed for the sport so hard, these women wouldn't be as at risk as they are, is all-consuming. Waves and waves of conflicting emotions used to eat away at me, and still do. I feel like I was too passionate and too naive. I didn't see that I was being used to paint an image of freedom and change that didn't truly exist. I was contributing to the smokescreen that masked the much more complex political and military developments in Afghanistan from the world. Realising not only that everything you've fought for – everything you've worked for and everything you've built – has disappeared in a flash, but that you have been used, is soul-destroying, regardless of the impact we were able to have on a personal level in the lives of individual players.

I once asked some players whether they wished they had never got involved in football. They said yes. That was a hard thing for me to hear. These women had fought for the right to play, as I had. They had used football as a tool to fight back against their oppression as women. They had put their lives at risk – crossing borders into the unknown and leaving everything, including many of their family members, behind – but they cannot formally be recognised as a national team.

A women's team would have to be sanctioned by the Afghanistan Football Federation, something which, under Taliban rule and influence, it will never do. So no team can exist. And FIFA? Instead of viewing this situation as an opportunity, a chance to change the rules and use football to push back against one of the most oppressive regimes in the world by taking a stand for women's rights and equality and backing these powerful and brave women, FIFA is unwilling to step up.

But when I walked around that room in Melbourne and embraced that team of women, when I looked them in the eyes and saw the determination in their faces, I knew that it didn't matter if FIFA hadn't understood yet. They would in time.

I watched the team meet Malala Yousafzai, a hero to women around the world. Initially I had been sceptical of Malala's interest in our story, so jaded was I by the opportunism of many people who have come forward in support over the years. But our shared enemy, the Taliban, and my and my sisters' lives of struggle against the oppressive regime, united us.

Malala has a beautiful soul. She was close in age to the players, and the similarities between the traumas they had all been through made it easy for the team to identify and connect with her. It was natural. She was able to interact with them and me in a way that very few others can. She spoke to the players, not like they were refugees, or broken and in need of help, but as people, as fighters, as sisters.

Despite her own trauma Malala has not turned her back on her cause, just as the players and I haven't either. And she did not turn her back on the team after an article or photo opportunity. Instead, she continues to champion the voices of the players.

I sat watching the game with the team. I listened to them shouting and laughing, appreciating a piece of skill. I could see the connection between them: the magic of a team in action, of trust in each other. The magic of football isn't really about the game. It's about something that the game unlocks that's already there: a connection, a belief in the shared purpose of the team. The beauty of that purpose.

There is the ball and there is you. But what really matters, is you.

Afterword

I never wanted to tell my story. I have been asked many times and each time I've held back, hesitated, even cringed at the idea. I feel the same way every time I am presented with an award. I immediately give them to my mother, and they sit on a shelf below the TV in her apartment in Denmark. I have never wanted them around me, and I don't want to see them. This is partly because I feel a trophy means that this is the end of something, and I have always been desperate for this story to be the beginning. But it is also because I feel allergic to anything that centres me – this is not about me, this is about all of us.

I am just one example, one person, one story within a larger society of many that we must reckon with. Consequently, I have always been uncomfortable with the fact that if I wrote a book it would inevitably have to have me at the centre of it, and I never wanted to portray myself as a hero. Heroes make doing the right thing seem somehow magical, something only a special category of human is capable of. It relieves other people of the obligation to change the world for the better by framing these achievements as unattainable unless you're an exceptional person. This is the story of my sisters and I fighting against the broken systems that failed to protect us. Those systems exist in every country around the world, and they harm all of us. We must always focus on the larger picture, not on individuals.

In recent years, however, I have started to change my mind about the value of stories. I have come to understand that people need them to make sense of the world, and those of us who are lucky enough – through accident or circumstance – to be able to tell our stories must not hide from that duty.

I was lucky because I had a family who valued me and my voice and were willing to sacrifice everything for my right to use it. I made decisions in the knowledge of what might happen to me, but my family were unfortunately forced on that journey without a choice. I agonise to this day over whether it was worth what we had to give up. How can I possibly balance this life against a world where my brother Idris would have still been alive? Where I might have been an aunt to his children? There are no words to tackle this.

As things currently stand, it is unlikely that I will ever be able to go home. I will probably never stand in our garden and smell the roses my grandfather planted. Writing this book has made that even more unlikely. It will increase the already daily calls for me to be raped, beaten and killed. I know that men and women in Afghanistan are far more likely to see me as abhorrent than worthy of celebration. I have scars that are still healing, and perhaps they never will. But all of us who live in exile must shoulder the burden of speaking up to raise awareness of the women who now live under brutal Taliban rule, to send them a message that they will not be forgotten. We must fight for them in whatever way we can, wherever we may be. We cannot be crippled by our guilt at surviving. We must take every opportunity to raise our voices and tell our stories. But we must also remember that those of us who survived, who have voices to speak, are a minority. Behind us, in the shadows, stand the hundreds and thousands of women who weren't so lucky. Whose voices will never be heard.

By now you know some of them. Dahmina was lost to the flames because that was better than the alternative. Samira was cut off from everything she loved by her family. Maryam was forced to flee from everything she knew.

And behind them are the stories of the women I dare not name because of the danger it would put them in. They have the right to anonymity, a right to decide whether their faces, names and trauma become public knowledge and how to tell their stories. Many of them have families that are still in Afghanistan and in grave danger, living in circumstances where their rights – to an education, to work, to leave the house without a male relative – have been stolen from them, where they are forced to bury themselves beneath burqas and scarfs. Some have had male family members killed or are single mothers trying to provide for their families without a male relative to support them or escort them to shops. They have a choice: punishment or starvation. For these reasons I have chosen to change the names of many of the women in this book. In some cases I have created composite characters, combining the stories of multiple women, to protect them from being identifiable. This was, sadly, not difficult to do, because so many of these women, myself included, have hugely similar, overlapping stories. But they remain a fraction of the whole.

Behind these stories are the sisters, aunts, grandmothers and mothers who willingly or unwillingly went along with the threats against their female relatives, either because they were terrified or because they were desperate for those crumbs of power and agency that were allowed to fall to them. Or because they had internalised the rules of a society that forces women to aggressively police the behaviour of each other. I will never judge those women; they face unimaginable choices every day just to survive. They may not know the word 'patriarchy', but they know that they live in a world framed by violence, where their lives are simply worth less than those of men. The past, present and future of women in Afghanistan are currently being erased: their struggles, stories and lives are veiled like the burqas they are forced into wearing. Every day this system continues should be cause for outrage.

And behind the women of Afghanistan are the millions of women in other countries around the world, a great chorus of unheard voices crying out in pain, sadness and fear, voices who need someone to speak up for them. So many voices you will never hear. Perhaps more than can be listened to.

But the fact that you are reading these words means you have found my voice and my story. And if I have done what I set out to do with this book, you will have had glimpses into the lives of some of the sisters I have known. You will hopefully have felt sadness, hope, despair, but also anger at the unfairness they have faced, at what was taken away from all of us by a repressive regime who assigns a different value to the lives of men and women. I want you to take that anger and remember that this is not happening at a safe distance.

Can you, wherever you are sitting reading this, honestly say the same is not true of your society? The men may not be holding machine guns and the women may not be in burqas, but whether it's reproductive healthcare, beauty standards, medical practices, wage inequality, unpaid care work or sexual violence, can you truly say you live in a fair society? Patriarchal society seeks to divide us, to pit us against each other, to stop us from uniting against systems that deny us. Together we are powerful. Together we are a team.

I have come close to breaking many times, sitting on a harbour wall and staring into the darkest water. The smallest of kindnesses have pulled me back from the edge. If you can see, every time that someone talks about refugees and displaced people as numbers or statistics, that those numbers are made up of hundreds and thousands of stories like mine, then perhaps you will feel just a little more kindly towards those who are vilified and scapegoated by the media and politicians. Because we can do terrible things to abstract numbers, things we would not be able to do to people.

The battle is to constantly remind ourselves that the world is made up of people, not statistics. When I travel the world, watching the power that football has to collapse those abstractions, it is the same joy, the same life, the same humanity, whichever country I am in. The same game. It is the message that FIFA uses to generate billions of dollars a year. But just because it has become a marketing slogan doesn't mean it isn't also true.

I have seen for myself what happens when women and girls are given the chance to play. I want to continue to be there for them, with my activism and the programmes that Girl Power supports, wherever they are in the world. Especially if they are refugees or displaced people. I know from first-hand experience how chaotic that life can be and how anything that offers any sense of stability and normality can be transformative. We all have it within us to be the person who reaches out with a small moment of kindness to bring someone back from the darkness.

There is a time, when you are part of a team, when you are losing, when you feel like you can't give any more, when you are dead on your feet, but you look around at your team and see in their eyes that they are not done yet, that you aren't finished. And you take strength from that, and you realise that you are not done yet either. It is my dream that this book might act like that for even one reader. I am not done yet. *We* are not done yet.

We will never stop being a nuisance. We will never stop poking and prodding. We will never stop asking for the rights that should be ours. We will never stop calling out hypocrisy where we see it. We will never stop asking, 'Why not us?' We will never stop running and running and kicking and shouting. Because there is the ball and there is you. But what really matters, is you – and your sisters, your team.

Acknowledgements

It's difficult to know who to thank first, so much of my story and the story of this team wouldn't have existed without many extraordinary people doing extraordinary things.

To begin, this book is for the players of the Afghanistan women's national team, which formally existed from 2007 to 2022 and continues to fight for its existence. Many of my teammates will never be able to tell their stories and so many of them have been rendered voiceless by a viciously misogynistic system. In telling my story, I wanted to elevate theirs too, since so much of their fight will never be shared. In addition to the team, this book is for all the women of Afghanistan, in this time of crisis.

To my family and Russell Pakzad, for providing love, comfort and enabling me to be the person I am, a person that never gives up. I would not be here were it not for you all, my wins are your wins.

Thank you to the coaching staff that took on our team and believed in it. Kelly Lindsey, Haley Carter, Joelle Muro, and John DeWitt. They trusted and joined us on a voluntary basis to help grow our team in the most difficult of circumstances. Kelly, I love and admire you so much. You have coached me, mentored me, listened to me, guided me and trusted me, as a coach, a sister and a friend. You are the reason I look at the world the way I do, and I have grown as a leader because of your friendship.

To HRH Prince Ali of Jordan, for quietly helping me and many of the players as the team navigated the dangerous sexual abuse scandal and FIFA's investigation into it. Your support has saved lives and was given without any desire for recognition.

Lisbeth Trnka, Benno Anton Borup, Henrik Bang, Soren Schriver, and Mette Billenstein Schriver. Thank you for opening your arms and homes in Denmark and welcoming me as if I were a family member.

Freddie Jorgensen, thank you for being an amazing mentor, showing love and support and being an ear for hours and hours when I was frustrated, sad, broken and needed to share my hurt. You showed up and guided me through.

Thank you to my Right to Dream and FC Nordsjaelland colleagues for supporting me, standing by my side and providing help, support and space during both the sexual abuse case and evacuation of players. To CEO Tom Vernon and his wife Helen, few workplaces would support their employee so fully, thank you too, for becoming family.

Hummel and Karma and their leaderships, in particular Hummel's Christian Stadil, deserve thanks for supporting me and the women of Afghanistan in every fight the team fought. When I needed them most, they showed up for us.

FIFPRO, the global players' union. You stood with us and advocated for justice, for me and my sisters. I am so grateful to you as an organisation, and for being the path for me to connect with so many strong role models and leaders. Former general secretary Jonas Baer-Hoffmann, human rights lawyer Kat Craig, director of global policy and strategic relations for women's football Sarah Gregorius and so many others who have supported me and the players beyond expectation and imagination.

Minky Worden, Human Rights Watch, Mary Harvey and the Centre for Sport and Human Rights, you have backed us and fought for us at every turn. To former Australian international and human rights advocate Craig Foster, former Olympian and human rights lawyer Nikki Dryden, director of Human Rights for All Alison Battisson and Melbourne Victory for helping with the evacuation of the senior national team and supporting them in building new lives in Australia. To Malala Yousafzai, for your unwavering support for the team, our battle against our shared enemy and your support in me telling my story.

To Leeds United chairman Andrea Radrizzani, Rabbi Moshe Margaretten, the Tzedek Association and Kim Kardashian for your commitment and support during the evacuation.

The Girl Power team, for going above and beyond to support me and our vision, you give me energy.

To Suzanne Wrack for helping me navigate getting this story onto paper, and to her and her colleagues at the *Guardian* for championing the struggles of women's football players in Afghanistan and holding truth to power. To my agents Max Edwards, Sara O'Keeffe and the team at Aevitas Creative, and to Lauren Howard and all the team at John Murray Press for bringing this book to life.

There will never be enough words for the thanks necessary. The football community rallied round the team and me. Countless people have saved my life and the lives of my sisters. So, thank you to everyone who has supported us, and thank you dear reader for supporting us by reading this story.